GERMAN ROMANTICISM AND
PHILIPP OTTO RUNGE

PHILIPP OTTO RUNGE   *Self Portrait in Brown Jacket*

1809/1810, oil on oakwood
48×47 cm.
H. K. Inv. No. 1005

GERMAN ROMANTICISM AND
PHILIPP OTTO RUNGE

A STUDY IN NINETEENTH-CENTURY

ART THEORY AND ICONOGRAPHY

Rudolf M. Bisanz

NORTHERN ILLINOIS UNIVERSITY PRESS

DeKalb: 1970

To my wife Ingeborg

CONTENTS

LIST OF ILLUSTRATIONS

Acknowledgments

I wish to express my appreciation to Dr. Victor Miesel of the University of Michigan for initially directing my attention to the need for an investigation of Runge in American scholarship. I thank Drs. William Fleming and Herbert Peisel, both of Syracuse University, for constant and cheerful encouragement and Dr. Sidney Thomas of the same university for his generous aid and criticism while I was engaged in the writing of an earlier draft of the manuscript. I further wish to acknowledge my indebtedness to Dr. Alfred Hentzen of the Hamburg Kunsthalle for his kind offer of assistance as well as his library and archive staff for their friendly cooperation. I am grateful to Drs. Christian Isermeyer and Wolfgang Schöne, both of the Kunsthistorisches Seminar of the Universität Hamburg, for stimulating suggestions based on their own distinguished work in Runge scholarship. My year's research in Germany was largely financed by a Fulbright Fellowship Grant. Without the untiring help as typist and the faithful, loving inspiration provided by my wife Ingeborg Bisanz, this book would not have come to being.

GERMAN ROMANTICISM AND
PHILIPP OTTO RUNGE

INTRODUCTION

*T*HE history of the arts and ideas of the nineteenth century, a period which had previously received fairly scant notice from art historians, has during the past twenty years attracted a remarkably high degree of scholarly attention on both sides of the Atlantic Ocean. Whatever the causes for this upsurge may be, as a result a large number of books and articles in the history of nineteenth-century art and its related or corroborative disciplines have been published lately, thereby alleviating the comparative dearth in our preceding systematic intelligence regarding that once somewhat neglected century. Yet, in spite of this very lively burgeoning of scholarly activity, it appears that very much still seems to have eluded us in our penetration of the epoch. As recently as 1966, Rudolf Zeitler in his monumental work entitled *Die Kunst des 19. Jahrhunderts* (The Art of the Nineteenth Century) felt impelled to christen summarily that century which stands chronologically so close to us and from which vast quantities of documentary information remain for our investigation, the "unknown century."

German Romanticism, or, more specifically, Early German Romanticism of approximately the last decade of the eighteenth and the first two decades of the nineteenth centuries, was a period of supreme seminal significance for the entire subsequent course of developments in German art and culture until the "Secessions" of the 1890s and the "Brücke" association of artists of 1905. Yet, contrary to what might be expected of occurrences lying in so recent a past, it opens up a wider hiatus in our understanding of the nature of events than any other movement affecting the course of art history during the nineteenth century.

As for the position of the American student of art history in relation to that particular period, the problem is doubly weighted in his disfavor: first, by the language barrier and its consequent effects of diminishing investigative vigor; and second, by the prevailing habit of American

scholarship and especially teaching to consign almost the entire continuation of the so-called Grand Tradition in art during the nineteenth
century to the nearly exclusive domain of France. All too often, certain
German artists—for example, Spitzweg, Leibl, Thoma, Busch, Menzel
or von Marées—are thus worthy of mention only by virtue of particular
traits of French naturalistic, Impressionistic, or Post-Impressionistic style
tendencies characterizing parts of their oeuvres instead of being subjected
to a general evaluation on the basis of their individual contribution to,
inventiveness, and uniqueness in German art as such. Some recent developments, however, are encouraging in that they attempt to check this
practice by evaluating the art of other nationalities during that period on
its own intrinsic merits, regardless of its affinities or lack thereof to a
"Grand Tradition" presumed to have been operative in French art during
the nineteenth century.

Nevertheless, while nearly all agree that a supranational cultural
"renascence" affecting variably almost all nations of the Western world
followed in the wake of a contagion loosely and by common consent termed
"romanticism," no conclusive theory has yet been offered to provide us
with an effective common denominator to deal with a vast multitude of
"romanticisms" despite many tentative hypotheses advanced to that end.
Consequently, a position opting for the systematic evaluation of a myriad
of determinants and phenomena constituting this amorphous semantic
denotation on the basis of causes and effects peculiar to each individual
nation or part thereof should have found a widespread consensus. Yet, it
has not, in spite of some adherence to the doctrine of pluralism laid down
in Lovejoy's brilliant essay "On the Discrimination of Romanticisms" and
in the face of overwhelming empirical evidence substantiating that choice.
If it had, the notion of a linear progress or direct advance in art, and therefore the continued presence of a "main course" in nineteenth-century art,
would have vanished as a result or at least would have been derogated to a
mere expression of current taste and fashion.

A circumspect and critical history of art dealing with the nineteenth
century will not fail to validate pluralism as the only appropriate aesthetic
modus operandi. The presence of strong forces of nationalism operating to
the decided detriment of a "spiritual internationalism" caused G. W. F.
Hegel to recognize in unremitting nationalism as Philosophy of State the
cardinal dilemma besetting international concord. He considered that
philosophical predicament insurmountable on logical grounds. It is consistent with logic also to deal with the art of the "Century of Nationalism"
on the same discriminatory basis, namely, one that is cognizant of the
presence of inconsistency. That dichotomy centers in the mutually exclusive
spheres of native demands in contrast to artistic ones that transcended
national limits. Many German artists in the period under discussion con-

4

sidered that issue as a central and deeply gnawing problem. But it becomes perhaps nowhere more vexingly apparent than in the schism inherent in the Nazarene School program which sought for a "truly" German art in, of all places, Rome. Even so, while the underlying basic philosophical dichotomy could only have led to eventual political catastrophe, in art the sentiments attending nationalism helped foster some genuinely native expression, a lingering nostalgia for the Apennine Peninsula notwithstanding.

In Germany, some artists accomplished in the nineteenth century what generations of their predecessors had failed to achieve, namely to lay the basis for an authentically indigenous expression. Thus the nineteenth-century witnesses in Germany the tentative emergence of a truly "popular" content in art, one founded on the principles of a conditional hermeticism relative to foreign influences, responding to specifically German spiritual needs, and therefore one responsible only to a critical evaluation based on the unique character of these needs.

The prevalent creative method in painting centered in a philosophical idealism that was complemented by an aesthetic classicism. Practical elaboration frequently added a naturalistic flavor. The actual imagery was thus prevented from fully assuming an innate form commensurate with those most heartfelt emotional needs which sought their deliverance in a truly functional art. The spontaneous release of those indigenous spiritual reserves occurred in the early twentieth century. However, in spite of the presumed close affinity between Romanticism and a historicism running counter to functional expressive freedom, the ideational bridge connecting the Gothic with the age of Expressionism was laid by the artists of the "romantic century." (It appears that the terms "historicism" and "functionalism" can no longer be considered the "polar opposites" dividing the nineteenth and twentieth centuries. In fact, no agreement whatsoever can be reached about the meaning of those designations with regard to painting. That, at any rate, is the conclusion—a judgment in which I concur—reached by the international panel of art historians who met in Munich in 1963 with the specific intention of clarifying this problem. (Cf. N. Pevsner, H. G. Evers, M. Besset, L. Grote, *et al.*, *Historismus und bildende Kunst, Vorträge und Diskussion.*)

The immediate impulse stimulating the needs for a native German expression in art—needs originating in the peculiar characteristics of German metaphysics—was brought about by the literature of the Storm and Stress period, by such early Romantic writers as Wackenroder, Novalis, Tieck, and Friedrich Schlegel, by the Jena School of Philosophy and such men as Fichte, Schelling, and Schleiermacher, as well as by the theoretical endeavors of such artists as Friedrich and Carus, but above all Runge.

That development of a relative exclusiveness, however, should not be construed as implying a qualitative derogation but, on the contrary, should point out the existence of a uniquely German temperament and conditions which precipitated and commanded a need for a certain artistic imagery to the detriment or exclusion of another. Thus, whatever imagery prevailed was historically also the only possible one to have existed at all. Viewed from that deceptively truistic perspective, the oeuvre of a Schwind, Richter, or Spitzweg, for example, will yield considerably more than merely quaintly anecdotal interest. The immense popularity it enjoyed and still enjoys even today should certainly be indicative of the artists' effective response to a common German need. That fulfillment, however, must not necessarily, as is done so often, be deprived of genuineness and artistic authenticity to satisfy an aloof aesthetic sophistication of *ars gratia artis*; particularly not when it is paired, as is the case with Schwind and Spitzweg, with a technique and style that rivals the great masters of draftsmanship and illusionistic realism.

The question, then, whether people command events or whether the two stand in an inverted relationship to each other might legitimately be asked in our context. It was Johann Gottfried Herder who said that whatever happens in the domain of mankind according to the measure of the ordained circumstances of national time and place does indeed happen historically. Applied to criticism in art, that view would certainly command a qualitative evaluation based on the principles of pluralism, nominalism, and personalism and indeed would require the discrimination of romanticisms. Heinrich Heine already noted the disparity between the spirits animating German as opposed to French Romanticism: he felt that the primordial Forest Ghosts of Germany would send the natty Boulevardier Ghosts of France scurrying into the night screaming in terror.

Conversely, Wellek's "unified theory" expressed in his *Romanticism in Literary History*, by searching for a common ground and coherency for "all romanticisms" in the nineteenth century, encourages many to seek also a "major line of development" in that theoretically existent functional unit of an incipient, homogeneous, supranational cultural "mass." When actually dealing with the term "romanticism," however, we are confronted with a vicious circle semantically, where neither the object's aggregate meaning can be induced from its constituent parts, nor these parts be deduced from the collective. Thus, in order to avert a further advance in a cul-de-sac, the search for a new nomenclature putting to rest "romanticism" as an unfunctional unit designation, seems imminent. Also, no objective defense can be advanced for the notion of evolutionary "progress" or advance in the art of any period above and beyond what Zeitler succinctly terms "partial causality" in the operation of influences.

In view of these unmitigable circumstances it is logical to disavow the practice of assessing qualitatively the art of the nineteenth century on grounds other than each artist's singularity as an individual human being,

6

the sincerity and comparative peculiarity of his ideational posture, the relative uniqueness of his personal style, the degree of his conditional expressive "functionalism," and the measure of his elective affinity to the spirit of an ethnic, religious, philosophical, regional, or national group. If grounds exist for assuming in addition also supranational cross-influences and those issuing from a conditional "historicism" or conditional "electicism" to affect his collective makeup, then these should be explored separately and on the basis only of specific data peculiar to him as an individual artist rather than on grounds which force his integration into a preconceived, at times highly doubtful, at times wholly unfunctional, configurational *gesamt*-structure.

Thus my position represents pluralism, personalism, and a qualified or conditional nominalism, one that proceeds from no single universal concept with regard to romanticism in the nineteenth century other than that which presumes the existence of a multitude of disparate causes affecting an equal number of heterogeneous responses. Conversely, the evaluation of any one given nineteenth-century artist should avoid an atomist approach but endeavor to synthesize a stylistic personality *Gestalt* qualified by the "partial causality" of objectively determinable elective affinities and influences.

Philipp Otto Runge's position of prominence as the central artist of that period known as Early Romanticism in Germany is undisputed by scholars. Yet no consensus has been reached about the exact nature, scope, and magnitude of Runge's original and lasting contribution. The controversy centers in the extent to which Runge may be given credit for having realized empirically the consequences of his comprehensive and ambitious visionary writings laid down in his *Hinterlassene Schriften*. However, the discussion is hindered from reaching conclusive results by an unfortunate but prevalent confusion of essentially disparate categorical relevancies—those of art practice and art theory; these two contingencies are, in the opinion of this writer, demonstrably divergent from each other in the case of Runge.

Runge's most interesting, emphatic, and challenging statements were posited by him in writing and not on canvas. Therefore, it is necessary to subject his theoretical writings to the scrutiny of a concentrated analytical effort unhampered by that unproductive controversy. While Runge's oeuvre has found very extensive recognition in numerous monographs, no inclusive attempts have been made to summarize in concise form the requisite, salient, historically original, and currently valid and stimulating features of his unorganized and informally written theories. My study represents an attempt at such a summary. Neither Runge's unique art nor his imaginative writings have found a response even nearly commensurate with their importance in the scholarship of the English-speaking world.

The procedure I have used can be termed biographical. In the main my method involves a critical, interpretive textual analysis of Runge's collected writings. His position as theorist is evaluated in the context of the general ideational milieu set by contemporary events in history, religion, philosophy, literature, and art and prevailing at the turn of the eighteenth into the nineteenth century. Runge's relationship to numerous personalities, specific movements, and currents characterizing the culture of the Napoleonic era is developed by me in detail and particularly with regard to Germany. My discussion is held in reference to and against the background of over sixty years of modern Runge scholarship.

My study attempts to demonstrate that a full appreciation of Runge's theory can only be gained if its evaluation is held separate from the critique of his art. It also exemplifies that Runge's art does not nearly exhaust the rich potential for revolutionary changes immanent in his theory. The discussion of Runge's major paintings and drawings is warranted by the burden of proof imposed by that argument and also by the current lack of information about them in America. Furthermore, my study shows that Runge combines in his writings nearly all of the most serious and profound features of Early German Romanticism in the areas of religion, philosophy, and literature and that he brings to bear these attitudes and sentiments in the most extensive document existing in German letters delineating the methods and aims of Romanticism in art. Moreover, it demonstrates that Runge's creative mind intuited, anticipated or, not seldom, literally pre-empted important developments of late nineteenth- and twentieth-century aesthetics and art pedagogy, in general, as well as significant theoretical aspects of Symbolism, Expressionism, and nonobjective abstract art, in particular. Conversely, it will be seen that he anticipated Impressionism in his own practice of painting.

Many decades have passed since the close of the nineteenth century and the "discovery" of Philipp Otto Runge after almost ninety years of nearly total obscurity. Since then the huge numbers of books, treatises, and articles which have been published about him often hail the artist as one of the greatest creative geniuses of the German nation. However, despite his growing posthumous fame and the rising proliferation of literature about him, an exhaustive "definitive assessment" of the famous romanticist's original contribution to art and art theory has neither been attempted nor has anything resembling a scholarly consensus been reached about it.

No doubt, that phase of research which subjected Runge to the scrutiny of analysis, dialysis, and deep quantitative probings seems to be drawing to a close. Now the wealth of objective data which have been compiled awaits careful weighing and sifting so that a qualitative summary or just such a "definitive assessment" of Runge's place and its importance in the history of art and ideas may be attained. So that such a comprehensive recept or synthesis of at least Runge's artistic theory, if not his whole oeuvre, may be realized, it is necessary to appraise critically—and against the background of over sixty years of scholarly opinion—Runge's extensive written testimony, deposited in his *Hinterlassene Schriften*, in its rambling entirety. More than a sufficient amount of pertinent material may thus be gleaned from the incipient mass which, if it is edited selectively and carefully evaluated, will be the single most eloquent witness to the intrinsic worth of Runge's "system." It is the purpose of this study to attempt such an appraisal, thereby demonstrating that Runge can indeed be given credit for the conception of a new romantic basis for and theory of art which by virtue of its originality, lasting value, and universal human relevancy stands as a cultural achievement of the first magnitude.

However, we should not discount in our calculations the possibility that in the instance of certain individuals, be they literary, philosophical, or artistic personalities, those elements which make up their collective images may be predicated on such a priori given premises as in their sum total could make group unanimity of opinion about them a virtual impossibility. The critique of Franz Kafka, for example, seems to have at last arrived at that point in history where the only agreement seems to be that there can be no agreement. It may very well be that a similar cardinal precept will be issued about Runge in the not too distant future.

Many scholars express the notion that Runge's theory should not be discussed in separation from his art, their assumption being that such an approach is detrimental to our concept of Runge's total contribution because it diminishes his importance as painter by reducing his "practical" output to a mere appendage of his theory. The direct result of this attitude has been that a summary assessment of Runge's art theoretical writings has not as yet been undertaken. But by the same logic it can be argued that an inordinate preoccupation with Runge's art should have precisely the opposite effect—that of unjustly diminishing the efficacy of his theory. We can readily see that such manner of argumentation leads us nowhere except into art history as comedy. But if we sharply distinguish at all times between Runge's ideas about art and his actual production of art, we will break the vicious cycle which has nearly incapacitated—and certainly has debilitated—Runge scholarship by constant attempts to explain Runge's theories on the basis of examples from his art and vice versa.

Actually, the efficacy of a given artistic theory can neither be invalidated by the failure of its originator to transform it into practice, nor can the worth of his practical oeuvre be discredited because of its deficiency in adhering to his professed theory. Works of art, after all, are autonomous entities which transcend all theory and can never be exhausted by any and all theorizing. Therefore, the manifest bifurcation of Runge's *Gesamtwerk* into theory and practice need not cause us any vexations at all, for each can be discussed separately and at its own proper time.

Thus my study is limited in scope to the discussion of Runge's theory of art and is based on the fundamental (if controversial) methodology which distinguishes sharply between theory and work. It attempts to demonstrate the identity of that theory as a revolutionary system of, and ideational approach to, art which stands as an original departure in history and as a lasting monument to its originator regardless of his factual artistic production. I trust that the following effort, brief though it is, will prove to be of value at this juncture of Runge scholarship by summarizing the essential "Runge as theorist" and thereby contributing in some measure to an eventual comprehensive synthesis of his total oeuvre. Beyond that—because of the absence of *Hinterlassene Schriften* in translation and because of the nearly total lack of relevant biographical material on Runge in English—the introduction of this central German romanticist to the American reader may be considered an additional modest contribution.

I have organized the complex material according to a model of concentric circles, whereby Runge's Christian faith can be visualized as forming the nucleus (Chapter I). His artistic credo (Chapter II) and his collective "theory" (Chapter III) represent the two subsequent circles. Chapters IV and V, dealing with Runge's color theory and iconography can be seen as the two outer rings. But because nearly all of Runge's statements are intimately connected with each other and thematically ambiguous, it is often impossible to determine their proper "heading" or "rubric" of subject and content. Therefore, my ordering should be regarded as only an approximation of the desirable in the context of a disputation. But if I have avoided the all too common pitfalls of rumination, prolixity, and the dispersal of arbitrary profundities about Runge, my organization has served at least a limited purpose.

My study is based principally on Runge's collected writings published by his oldest brother Daniel Runge as *Hinterlassene Schriften* von Philipp Otto Runge Mahler, herausgegeben von dessen ältestem Bruder (Verlag von Friedrich Perthes, Hamburg, 1840/1, I–II, 435 + 554 pp.). The edition used is Philipp Otto Runge, *Hinterlassene Schriften* (facsimile printing of the edition of 1840/1, Vandenhoeck and Ruprecht, Göttingen, 1965, I–II). Quotations appearing hereafter are those of Runge unless they are otherwise indicated. The abbreviation *H.S.*I, p. 1 will be used in the references to indicate pagination. By far the most important source pertaining to Runge's biography is "Nachrichten von dem Lebens- und Bildungsgange des Mahlers Philipp Otto Runge" (*H.S.*II, pp. 441–512). Further biographical material may be found in Heinrich Steffen's *Was ich* *erlebte* (München, 1956, pp. 210 ff.); Johann Georg Rist, *J. G. Rists Lebenserinnerungen* (I–II, Gotha, 1880); C. T. Perthes, *Friedrich Perthes' Leben nach dessen schriftlichen und mündlichen Mitteilungen* (I–II, Gotha, 1857). In "Kritiken und Berichte" (*H.S.*II, pp. 513–554), Daniel compiled most of the published critical judgments about Runge's oeuvre as of the year 1841. For an overview of the most significant works of Runge scholarship, the reader is referred to the "Selected Bibliography" at the end of this study where works containing bibliographies are so indicated. All citations I have used in this study are included in full in the bibliography at the end of the book; for this reason, short titles have been used in the text.

Gustav Pauli's paragraphs on Philipp Otto Runge in *Propyläen Kunstgeschichte, XIV, Die Kunst des Klassizismus und der Romantik* (Berlin, 1925, pp. 96 ff.) and P. F. Schmidt's article "Philipp Otto Runge" in Thieme-Becker *Künstlerlexikon* (1935) are the best general introductions to the study of Runge. Hamburg Kunsthalle in Hamburg, Germany, contains nearly the total of Runge's artistic oeuvre.

In view of the great importance attributed to Runge by German art historians, it is indeed quite astonishing to note that English and American scholarly involvement in the study of Runge is conspicuous by its virtual absence. The only contributions of substance are to my knowledge those by J. B. C. Grundy and O. G. v. Simson. While Simson's article, written in 1942, is remarkable for the immense erudition of its author and Grundy's essay of 1930 noteworthy for the lack of incisive comprehension of its subject, both deal with special and peripheral topics, thus skirting a central issue, namely the over-all exposition and appraisal of Runge's contributions for the American reader. (My frequent references to Runge's art are prompted chiefly by my desire to "round out the picture" for him.) The inclusion of three of Runge's letters in English translation, in Elizabeth Holt's anthology *From the Classicists to the Impressionists* of 1966, is worthy of mention and praise.

A word on my translation of Runge's writings is advisable. A number of circumstances—Runge's lack of a sustained formal education, the carelessness of composition characterizing much of his private correspondence, his obvious inability to express the effusive gush of his thoughts and ideas in reasoned and measured syntax, along with his prepossession in favor of metaphorical conjunction and allegorical representation—tend to make his German prose all too often appear overly enthusiastic, headlong, and very difficult to understand, even for a German. Regardless of Runge's stylistic and technical shortcomings, and perhaps partly because of them, his writings evince a sense of personal enthusiasm and exuberant commitment for the things in which he believed and move the contemporary reader with the same feeling of urgency and excitement in which they were conceived.

I. PREMISES

*P*HILIPP OTTO RUNGE was born the ninth of eleven children of a shipowner and businessman in Wolgast, Swedish Pomerania, on July 23, 1777, and died in Hamburg on December 2, 1810. His parents were of peasant stock, and their conduct of daily affairs permeated the household with the sincere piety of the Lutheran faith based on catechistic principles. His oldest brother Daniel writes: "In our house reigned through the disposition of our parents—our mother's having been more leisurely and even poetic, our father's ruled by a sharp mind—the spirit of an unpretentious piety, which, adhering simply to the Bible and the catechism in diligent practice, became rooted in the mind of our Otto as a quiet perpetual impression" (*H.S.*II, p. 444). The spirit of a heartfelt solidarity united all members of the large family intimately and constantly throughout Runge's life and provided him with the mainstay of solace during times of grief. Twice in his youth, Runge was seriously ill and his life was in danger. A weak and sickly child, he made the least progress in school of all his brothers and sisters, although, endowed by nature with a joyous spirit, he participated vivaciously in all children's games (*H.S.*II, p. 444). On his eighteenth birthday, the family decided to apprentice him in the shipping and provision company of his brother Daniel in Hamburg. Prior to his departure, his artistic talents, which he demonstrated chiefly in skillful silhouettes, were recognized and fostered by his teacher and mentor, the poet-theologian Theobul Kosegarten, who counseled on behalf of an academic career for his protégé against the expressed wishes of Runge's father, who took a rather dim view of university life and higher education.

The influence of Theobul Kosegarten on the young Runge is a special object of concern for Gunnar Berefelt's study entitled *Philipp Otto Runge zwischen Aufbruch und Opposition 1777–1802* (pp. 21 ff.), and the summary of his finding appears on page 39. Berefelt, however, ascribes to him an importance which is not corroborated by many biographers of Runge. Kosegarten's contribution to German letters is negligible. His was not an original mind. There is no mention of him in Haym's *Die Romantische Schule*, Kluckhohn's *Das Ideengut der Deutschen Romantik*, or Fritz Martini's *Deutsche Literaturgeschichte*, all works regarded as classical standard texts. Benz ascribes to Kosegarten as "a poet of idylls originating in Voss" an "inclination toward nature enthusiasm, even toward idealized Germanic heroism, toward the Spheres of Ossian and the Night Thoughts of Young" (*Die Deutsche Romantik*, p. 179). It is generally agreed that Kosegarten's major influence on Runge was to have introduced the boy to pietistic and nature lyricism and to aspects of the early English Romantic literature.

Upon his arrival in the Hanseatic city, Runge was received by the circle of his brother's friends who, according to Daniel, had entered upon a "romantic friendship pact" that was characterized by "a strong inclination toward reading and mutual communication of mostly poetical and philosophical writings of the present and the past" (*H.S.*II, p. 447). When not occupied with his menial office duties, Runge participated in the lively intellectual discussions which marked the challenging atmosphere surrounding the Hamburg milieu.

The Hamburg coterie centered around Daniel consisted of members of that small enlightened middle-class group which, while pursuing their daily activities in publishing, business, and the professions, participated vigorously in the contemporary artistic and intellectual dialogue, often enriching it with their own creative contributions. Speckter, Hülsenbeck, Wülffing, Besser, Perthes, Herterich, Hardorff were some of the principal names visiting the Runge household in Hamburg. The list of "guests and acquaintances" is sheerly endless. Some of these men made lasting imprints in the cultural heritage of Germany, and their names are intimately bound up with the German history of the Napoleonic era. Thus Runge entered, upon his arrival in Hamburg, also one of the principal "literary salons" of that city. He also kept close touch with the now perhaps more famous Claudius circle there. Inasmuch as Runge's proclivities were not for reading so much as for "learning through conversation," it is extremely difficult to isolate individual influences operative on him. With the wide dissemination of printed material at the turn of the century and Runge's predilection to acquire, nay devour, knowledge and information primarily through personal contact with well-read persons, and despite Runge's "rhetorical" admission never to have read a philosophical tract in his whole life, it is safer to assume that he was familiar with any given leading ideas of the time than that he was not. (Cf. his letters to his brother Gustaf, Jan. 19, 1808, *H.S.*I, p. 208; to Böhndel, December 1801, *H.S.*II, p. 104; "Lebensgänge des Verfassers," *H.S.*II, p. 512; to F. W. J. Schelling,

February 1810, *H.S.*I, p. 157.) We should, therefore, not concern ourselves too much with the listing of the myriad of influences active upon
him, as his biographers so relentlessly do, but rather perhaps opt for the
much shorter list of "non-influences."

Increasingly more unhappy with his fledgling business career, Runge
found comfort in reading the classics as well as contemporary literature.
The study of the most important literary and philosophical journals of the
day, principally those edited by Schiller, Goethe, the Schlegel brothers,
and Claudius, introduced him into the main current of the contemporary
cultural dialogue.

Among the classics, he read the *Odyssey* in the translation by Voss,
the *Iliad*, translations of Virgil and Ovid, the Old Saxon *Reineke de Voss*
(*H.S.*II, p. 448). Chief among the contemporary literature to which
Runge was exposed were the following leading periodicals: (1) Friedrich
Schiller's *Horen* and *Musenalmanach* (published 1797–1800), two journals
on ethics, and the principal organs for the dissemination of the post-
Kantian principles centering in the ideals of freedom, duty, belief in im-
mortality and God as the chief ideational agents of moral conduct in the
framework of a new *Moralphilosophie* encompassing "natural philosophy"
and aesthetics and designed to attain the *schöne Seele* through grace, dignity,
and beauty. The salient features of Schiller's *Aesthetische Briefe über die
Erziehung des Menschen* of 1795 became thus also known to Runge in their
advocacy of an artistic elite providing "education toward beauty" and
"leadership in all spheres of life" (Martini, p. 269). Both Goethe and
Wilhelm von Humboldt cooperated on these periodicals. Through them
Runge became acquainted with the finest flower of German classical
humanism. (2) Goethe's *Propyläen* (founded in 1798 in cooperation with
the *Weimarer Kunstfreunde*), a journal on aesthetics in which were delineat-
ed the chief arguments of German Neoclassicism in art. These were
founded on the principles of Winckelmann and his epithet "Edle Einfalt,
stille Grösse," espousing the highest ideals of order, harmony, and
balance in art and standing in strict opposition to burgeoning Romantic
aesthetics. Runge became an enthusiastic *Propyläen* reader and avidly
adopted all its tenets germane to the subject, content, and style of art in
the "classic" manner. (For Runge's change in attitude vis-à-vis Neoclassicism and his break with the *Propyläen* program compare Chapter II.)
(3) Friedrich Schlegel's *Athenaeum* (published 1798–1800, in cooperation
with Wilhelm and Dorothea Schlegel, Novalis, Schleiermacher, Tieck, and
Schelling). The rival organ of the *Propyläen*, this journal on aesthetics
was the chief medium for the dissemination of the "Romantic point of
view" at the time of the movement's most compelling period of argumentation. All the important Romantic propositions advanced by the finest
advocates of the movement were familiar to Runge, as, for example,

Novalis's "Hymnen an die Nacht,""Blüthenstaub," "Die Christenheit oder Europa," Schlegel's poignant aphorisms in his "Fragmente" and Schleiermacher's Romantic-Pietistic pulpit sermons. (4) Mathias Claudius's *Wandsbecker Bote*, an organ for the "Christian-moral education of the home population" (Martini, p. 206) was a constant companion in the Runge household. The famous North German lyricist was also considered "part of the family" owing to Perthes's marriage to one of Claudius's daughters (*H.S.*II, p. 447). Runge can be regarded as belonging to the "Claudius circle." (5) Finally, the *Göttinger Hainbund* (Schubart, Bürger, Voss, Hölty, etc.) and its Sturm und Drang lyricism inspired by Klopstock, a poetry attended by irrationalism, sentimentalism, nature adulation, and religiosity.

The reading of Ludwig Tieck's hyper-romantic *Franz Sternbalds Wanderungen* was a major experience for Runge. Moved deeply by this archetypal Romantic "artist's novel," he exclaimed: "I have never been so stirred in my innermost soul as I have been by this book which the good T. has justifiably called his favorite child" (letter to Besser, June 3, 1798, *H.S.*II, p. 9).

In response to his urgent wishes, Runge was first allowed to take private art lessons in Hamburg and then to enter the art academy in Copenhagen, at that time one of the leading centers of Neoclassicism in Europe. In Hamburg Runge received lessons from Eckhardt, Herterich, and Hardorff, all minor practitioners of the artistic métier. Hardorff received his training from A. Tischbein and Casanova, therefore was a scion of the "grand" classical tradition of the expiring Baroque era. (For the most thorough treatment of Runge's early training and development to this date consult Berefelt, *Philipp Otto Runge*.) Runge's teachers in Copenhagen included Abildgaard, Wiedewelt, and the famous Jens Juel, whose tutoring introduced him to the best tradition of late Rococo portraiture practiced anywhere. Flaxman's contour drawings and probably also engravings of David's works stimulated Runge at Copenhagen. While most of Runge's time was spent in copying plaster casts, yet the little instruction in technique and the introduction to the plein-air "view landscape" which he did receive formed the basis for his subsequent independent study. There can be no question in my mind but that Runge's career suffered because of a lack of a prolonged and sustained training in technique. His increasing reliance on self-study cost him much wasted time, although it also bore rich fruit. A specific discussion of the academy at Copenhagen, which in Runge's days was the artistic mecca for the artists of the North German region, by Charlotte Hintze (*Kopenhagen und die Deutsche Malerei um 1800*) develops in detail the ideational climate in that artistic center during Runge's time. He attended classes for nearly two years (1799–1801) but, dissatisfied with the artistic climate in Copenhagen, he decided to relocate in Dresden, then the art capital of Germany, and to continue his training independent of academic tutelage.

The artistic milieu of Dresden was determined, among other things, by a renowned art academy (which fostered both Neoclassicism and late Baroque realism), by the gallery (which contained a superb collection including Raphael's *Sistine Madonna* and Correggio's *Night Nativity*, both influential on Runge), a sizeable antique sculpture collection, the Mengs Collection, and one of the finest copper engravings libraries of the old masters available anywhere. Runge made extensive use of these resources while widening his art historical horizon. For Runge's critical appraisal of the academy professors reference is made to his letter to Böhndel, of Dec. 18, 1801 (*H.S.*II, pp. 102 ff.). While severely criticizing Grassi, he lauds Klengel and Mechau, both of whom have achieved a lasting reputation as landscape artists. On the whole, however, Runge was disillusioned by the ideational atmosphere (or lack of it) prevailing at the art academy. A friendly relationship developed between Runge and the amiable old Anton Graff, who made the young man a member of his family. Graff was a fine technician, and his lasting fame rests upon his unpretentious bourgeois portraiture in a classically objective style with a solid light construction and some Rococo traces. The influences of Juel and Graff upon Runge's own *Freilichtportraiture* are strong. Eberlein (*Runge's "Tageszeiten," Das Gesamtkunstwerk der Romantik*) summarily states that in Runge converge influences of "English classicism and French Empire, Italian Renaissance and Italian Baroque" as well as those of "Saxon Late Gothic," the last mentioned because Runge may have seen the unusual "Tulip Pulpit" of 1480 at the Cathedral of Freiburg although he never mentioned having visited there. However, he did write an enthusiastic letter describing his visit to the Cathedral of Meissen (*H.S.*II, p. 221). An additional interesting study concerning this particular problem is that by Neumann regarding the "Tulip Pulpit" influence on Runge's *Der Morgen*, entitled *Drei merkwürdige künstlerische Anregungen bei Runge, Manet, Goya*.

Soon after his arrival in Dresden, Runge met Tieck, and a close friendship ensued between the two men. For several decades during the twentieth century the Tieck-Runge scholarship faltered on the point of these two men's influences upon each other. It was assumed that Runge was a mere weak echo of the poet. Recent scholarship affirms cogently the strength of conviction and personal force of the artist with regard to his role as leader rather than follower in many instances which theretofore had been thought otherwise. Thus, today considerations of the Tieck-Runge relationship view affirmatively the latter's active contribution in the ideological dialogue between the two men, particularly in view of our knowledge of Tieck's rather weak or indecisive character. As the most pertinent special literature dealing with the problem should be noted J. B.

C. Grundy's *Tieck and Runge, A Study in the Relationship of Literature and Art in the Romantic Period with Special Reference to "Franz Sternbald"*; Sigfried Krebs's *Ph. O. Runge's Entwicklung unter dem Einflusse L. Tiecks*; and S. Krebs's *Philipp Otto Runge und Ludwig Tieck*.

Runge himself says the following about the relationship:

It is no accident but it must be so that I and Tieck most closely coincide in everything; I am even as the executive power, I was born to work and I am not happy if I cannot produce. Without Tieck I might perhaps delve into practice and virtuosity and get lost in them, just as Raphael has done it toward the end; and without my spoken contribution Tieck might get lost in his feelings: we both agree on that (letter to Daniel, March 1803, *H.S.*I, p. 38).

In later years Runge's feelings toward his friend cooled considerably, probably because of Tieck's espousal of Catholicism. It is generally agreed by all that Tieck's major contribution to the development of the artist was to have introduced him to his friend Novalis's writings (beyond Runge's previous knowledge of the early deceased poet's writings from his reading of *Athenaeum*), to have opened up for him the mystical world of Jacob Böhme, and to have initiated him into the ultra-religious-aesthetic atmosphere of Wackenroder's *Herzensergiessungen eines kunstliebenden Klosterbruders*. But no matter how strong the parallelisms among Tieck's, Novalis's, Wackenroder's and Runge's attitudes concerning the religious and philosophical mission of art may be, the written poetic and the visual artistic modes of expression differ so drastically in their basic elements of form as in effect to have left to Runge the task of re-inventing all symbolism for the imagery of art.

It is neither the task of this study to discuss Runge's actual realization of his theories, nor to become involved in the issues of "influences" on Runge with their attendant host of peripheral problems. Rather I want to demonstrate the creation by Runge of an art theory which is autonomous, potentially realizable into practice, and legitimately founded on its own intrinsic logic. Nevertheless, a fairly persistent shortcoming of much of the scholarly literature devoted to the discussion of "general problems affecting the arts" has been a lack of sufficient stress on the fundamental disparity of the different artistic modes of expression. This, it seems, is due to the inability of any one scholar to be equally well versed in the possibilities and limitations of several media; in the case of art historians it is unfortunately true that they often lack even a basic grounding in the specificities of the actual studio situation, that is, that very discipline which is the chief domain of their theoretical investigations. And even the most recent and significant Runge scholarship seems to falter on that critical point. Kenneth Negus observes this deficiency in his discussion of Curt Grützmacher's *Novalis und Philipp Otto Runge*: ". . . some will doubtless be disappointed at finding no discussion on differences between Novalis's and Runge's works, arising from the different arts concerned—writing and painting . . . at least a minimal amount of attention could well have been devoted to the two art media in their confrontation here" (*German Quarterly*, Spring 1966, pp. 242–243).

Runge also met Goethe in Weimar, an event which marked the beginning of a lifelong relationship based on their mutual interest in the theory of color, if not on kindred aesthetic persuasions. Goethe stood in direct opposition to Runge's Romantic allegorical art objectives. However, he recognized the full measure of the young man's genius and encouraged him in a friendly manner. Conversely, *Hinterlassene Schriften* are punctuated by Runge's caustic remarks about Goethe as well as by expressions of great admiration. Goethe neither helped further Runge's art and art theory nor did he contribute to his color theory beyond friendly words of encouragement. "I could not take anything from him [Goethe], I have told him many things, he has told me nothing . . ." (Runge's letter to Steffens, March 1809, *H.S.*I, p. 147). *Hinterlassene Schriften* contain the major bulk of the Goethe-Runge correspondence. Hellmuth Freiherr von Maltzahn's *Philipp Otto Runge's Briefwechsel mit Goethe* does not significantly add to our knowledge.

The year 1802 was marked by a succession of historic events in Runge's life which fundamentally shaped his remaining years. Principal among these were his stormy courtship of Pauline Bassenge (who in their happy marriage bore him four children, the youngest born the day after Runge's premature death), his rebuff at the Neoclassical art competition of the *Weimarer Kunstfreunde*, and the critical success of his *Triumph des Amor*.

Runge participated in 1801 in the annual art competition conducted by Goethe's *Propyläen* in collaboration with the *Weimarer Kunstfreunde*. His entry, based on the prescribed subject matter derived from the *Iliad*, is entitled *Achill im Kampf mit dem Flussgott Skamandros* (1801, pen and ink and gouache on brown paper, 53 × 67.2 cm., Hamburg Kunsthalle, inv. no. 34231). The work received a "disastrous" critique: "However the drawing cannot be considered good, it is wrong and mannered. We advise the author to study antiquity and nature seriously and in the spirit of the ancients. But above all he needs to consider the works of the great masters of all times" (*Allgemeine Literaturzeitung*, von 1802, "Weimarische Kunstausstellung von 1801"; compare *H.S.*II, pp. 513 f.). Chapter II will provide a detailed discussion of Runge's attitude during and after the Weimar rebuff.

Begun in Copenhagen, the project of *Triumph des Amor* went through several stages, the culmination of which is the painting of 1801/2 (oil on canvas, 66 × 173 cm., Hamburg Kunsthalle, inv. no. 2691). As an allegory on the cycles of love, comprising eighteen child figures, in the manner of a bas-relief, it witnesses Runge's full attainment of the classical idiom in art.

More important even than these events in Runge's career were the crystallization of his own Romantic art theory and the genesis of his cycle of drawings, the key work of his artistic oeuvre, entitled *Die Tageszeiten*. Both of these crucial developments occurred in the same year, and both will be discussed in considerable detail in chapters II and V.

Thus, at the early age of twenty-five, Runge had reached nearly all the basic artistic and ideational premises of his career, and the remaining eight years of his life were devoted to the continued expansion, elaboration, explanation, and completion of the precepts of 1802. Drawing increasingly the raptured attention of the Romantic coterie of Germany by the power of his personality, the uniqueness of his art, and the strength of his ethical, literary, and aesthetic beliefs, he became the nexus of the whole Early German Romantic movement during the ensuing years. Aubert bestows upon him the accolade of "the eye of Early German Romanticism" while referring to his circle of friends as the "central exchange of German Romanticism's period of flower." He continues: "Goethe and Tischbein, as the old Graff, Steffens and Tieck, Friedrich and Wilhelm Schlegel, with the last two mentioned Runge had a somewhat more reserved relationship, Rumohr, Görres, Arnim, Brentano, Jakob and Wilhelm Grimm, Schelling, Fichte—in the midst of the circle of such men stands Runge with his life's work" (*Runge und die Romantik*, pp. 23, 30). Schmidt suggests: "We will no longer be able to overlook (as have Haym and Ricarda Huch, to say nothing of others) that the period of flowering of Romanticism has found its fulfillment in the work of Runge" (*Philipp Otto Runge, Sein Leben und Sein Werk*, p. 56). Pauli summarizes: "All that Early Romanticism demanded of art, even the seeds to all that was as yet uncomprehended, but was later to sprout from the romantic movement, all that germinates and is to be found united in Runge" (*Die Kunst des Klassizismus und der Romantik*, p. 96). I could not hope to summarize Runge's relationship to the various Romantic personalities discussed better than Kleinmayr, who says: "Schlegel was a writer, Wackenroder a priest of painting and music, Tieck a poet; Runge combines their individual attitudes into a unified point of view. As religious man he is related to Schleiermacher, as poet-painter to Novalis-Tieck" (*Die Deutsche Romantik und die Landschaftsmalerei*). Those who knew Runge, all agree in their impressions and personal assessments of him: he was forceful, persuasive, dynamic, yet charming and humorous, easily the outstanding figure in any group or company. For individual assessments of Runge's personality, the principal "character witnesses" Daniel Runge, Tieck, and Goethe should be consulted in *Hinterlassene Schriften*. Further we should also refer to Rist, Steffens, and Perthes (op. cit). We notice in the accounts of these men the marked difference between Runge's character and that of C. D. Friedrich, the lonesome, eccentric, distrustful recluse. Yet both men were "artistic outsiders."

Although the last years of Runge's life were saddened by his deteriorating health, the dangers of the Napoleonic Wars which swept across Northern Germany, and the hardships of the Continental Blockade, which, particularly affecting the commerce of the Free State of Hamburg, forced him to come to the aid of his brother's faltering business in a selfless act of love, Runge did not cease to work relentlessly on the solution of many painting and design problems and, above all, to labor on his ambitious color theory and the execution of his major painting *Der Morgen*. The latter as part of the *Tageszeiten* cycle will be discussed at length in Chapter V.

Runge was yet allowed to witness the publication of his color theory, *Die Farbenkugel*, and the prior, partial adaptation by Goethe of some of his theories in the latter's *Farbenlehre*. (Compare "Die Farbenkugel betreffend. Aus Goethes: zur Farbenlehre, erster Band, S. 339," *H.S.*II, pp. 541 f. For the discussion of the common interest both men shared in the "science of color" and the relation of both to Newton, refer to Chapter IV. For a brief but caustic discussion of Goethe the scientist refer to Sherrington, *Goethe on Nature and on Science*. Sherrington deflates Goethe's *naturwissenschaftliche Versuche* with the sharp sting of modern science.)

On December 2, 1810, a violently progressive lung ailment snuffed out Runge's life at the age of thirty-three. It can be stated with certainty that Runge's disease was tuberculosis. His sickness "was nothing else but a quickly expanding consumption" (Daniel to Klinkowström in Rome, March 9, 1811, *H.S.*II, p. 428). An interesting study by Erich Ebstein (*Tuberkulose als Schicksal*) makes mention of Runge (pp. 101 ff.) in connection with the effect of the illness on the workings of creative fantasy, compulsive way of life, premonition of untimely death, and consequent haste in work habits, all symptoms which seem to be borne out by Runge's life and the tenor of *Hinterlassene Schriften*. Ebstein's thesis, however, maintains that, despite these effects, significant personalities who had suffered from tuberculosis created their work *despite* their illness; thus it attempts to disprove the "popular" theory that genius is "enhanced" by tuberculosis.

Shortly before Runge's death, Goethe wrote to the publisher Friedrich Perthes, Runge's lifelong friend: "He is one of those individuals who are seldom born. His superior talent, his true and faithful nature as artist and human being, has already for a long time aroused my affection and attachment; and if his direction diverted him from that road which I consider to be the right one, I was therefore not displeased, but I accompanied him willingly where his peculiar manner carried him" (Weimar, Nov. 16, 1810. *H.S.*II, p. 423).

Upon Runge's death his name fell into obscurity. The great promise of a new national school of art centered around the artist and led by his vigorous example remained unfulfilled during his lifetime. Several reasons may be given for this, for example, his residence outside of the major centers of artistic activity, the personal hardships caused by his ill health and the ravages of war, and, of course, his early death which prevented him from ever reaching the full potential of his creative powers. But the major reasons—even though this may sound very trite—seems to me that Runge was "too far in advance of his times to be accepted by them." It will become apparent in the body of this presentation that all the theoretical premises for a "new Romantic school of art" were laid down by Runge, but because of their great scope and complexity they could not be effective once the reformer himself was gone. Even if his fragmentary oeuvre had been widely known, it could not have been a decisive guideline for practicing artists, just as today it provides scholars with little more than the basis for heated controversies. Runge's art gives us only a glimpse of the enormous potential his theory held in store. *Hinterlassene Schriften*, had they been published immediately after Runge's death, could have been ever so much more effective than they were when they appeared, thirty years later and at a time when Romanticism's early fire had spent itself to glimmering ashes. The artist's memory was drowned in the roar of the times.

Runge stood at the crossroads of the expiring Baroque and the burgeoning modern art. The course he took was strangely his own. While close correspondences between his ideas and those of Schiller, Wackenroder, Novalis, Tieck, Friedrich Schlegel, Clemens Brentano, Schelling, Steffens, Schleirmacher, Mathias Claudius, and many others do exist, his theories and his art as such ultimately occupy a unique position in history. No close or kindred relationships (despite certain superficial similarities) can be established between Runge and the most noteworthy of his classically oriented predecessors and contemporaries in art, such as, for example, Mengs, Carstens, Wächter, Koch, Schick, Genelli, the Tischbeins, Chodowiecki, Angelica Kauffmann, Füger, or Krafft. Nor is Runge "related" to the Nazarenes and such men as Overbeck, Führich, Veit, Pforr, J. Carolsfeld, Koch, the Oliviers, the Schadows, who ventured to Rome and captured the imagination of wealthy patrons as well as the sympathy of the people with their pious, simplistic, introspective, intimate eclecticism in the manner of the late Quattrocento, while stimulating kindred movements in Vienna, Hamburg, and Berlin. These men began with a rejection of the international, classic-academic style, then adopted an "indigenously German style," only to revert in their final phases to what appears to be academicism and internationalism. (Just as puzzling was their attempt to find that "indigenously German style" in, of all places,

Rome!) One of them, Peter Cornelius, sought with his excellent drafts-manship, classical themes, and classical style the synthesis of Greek antiquity and Christianity, while laying the foundation of the Schools of Munich and Düsseldorf and thereby establishing for the remainder of the century in Germany the "Grand Tradition" in monumental fresco as well as easel painting.

The dominance of Munich and Düsseldorf over the German art scene may be regarded as the single most hostile impediment to Runge's objectives. Men such as Fohr, Genelli, Kaulbach, Stilke, Piloty, Rethel, and others perpetuated the successful Munich-Düsseldorf formula of equal parts of classicism, realism, and "romanticism" in great idyllic, historic, and religious productions, technical facility having been sufficient reason for other minor practitioners of the métier to engulf the public with mass-produced "studio machines" teeming with gods, nymphs, satyrs, medieval heroes, and occasional saints. The gulf between these productions, regard-less of our current assessment of them, and that which Runge sought in art widened perceptively and in proportion to the progressive materialization of art and the mundane spirit from which it emanated.

Also Rungian ideas about landscape seem nowhere to have found an echo. Only Friedrich and his circle, as we will see later on, represent an exception, although a highly disputable one. But the work of such men as Koch, Hackert, Gessner, Reinhart, Rottmann, Preller, Schirmer, Goethe, Oeser, Schütz, Klengel, Kobell, Rebell, and of other representative practitioners of the landscape genre, who either perpetuated the Poussin-Claude and Ruisdaelian formulae or else worked in the Dutch intimist tradition, had little in common with Runge's landscape objectives. The late and sometimes philistine Biedermeier Romanticism of such great artists as Spitzweg, Schwind, Richter, Rethel, and Steinle pictured with an infinite amount of detail and fidelity, in pleasing, narrative genre anecdotes the worlds of fairy tale, fable, and contented middle-class existence, to the delight of art afficionados recruited largely from the ranks of the very same bourgeoisie which that art depicted thematically. The Cornelian epigones and the mighty Late Romantic "idea painters," such as Feuerbach, Böcklin, von Marées, Thoma, Stuck, and others, once again in the later half of the century attempted, and often very successfully, to infuse the now thread-bare Biedermeier formulae with new life and vigor and authenticity. Finally, the Naturalism of Menzel and Leibl, the "impressionism" of the *Sezession* and such men as Lieberman, Slevogt, Uhde, and Corinth close off an era in German art history. Nowhere in this development, either theoretically or practically, were Runge's ideas followed, because of doctrinaire oppositions to his concepts or because of insufficient infor-mation about them or because of both reasons. Not until the proliferation of Post-Impressionist movements, Expressionism, and the twentieth century did artists begin working in analogy with the spirit or according to the letter of Runge's theories.

We can compare Runge to El Greco, who was quickly forgotten after his death only to rise like phoenix from the ashes to soaring heights of critical esteem in the twentieth century. We do not know the reasons for this, but we can speculate about them. It seems that in the instance of certain artists, for example, Runge, Van Gogh, El Greco, Bosch, Grünewald, an ideational affinity, a *Wahlverwandtschaft*, a world-historical analogy must first exist between the vision these artists held of their world and that of their "discoverers" of their own times for these artists to be recognized and evaluated in the full measure of their intrinsic worth. It is a moot point indeed who comes first in this process. Whether it is the artist, working in and for his time, driven by dynamic forces beyond his control that animate the culture of his epoch, who stumbles unwittingly and unintentionally upon historical analogies—which he may not recognize as such or may not care to know about at all—and is then "linked" to "predecessors" by watchful art historians and critics; or whether the crafty art historians come first with their insights, only to be exploited by practicing artists for the full measure of their critical acumen. I rather tend to choose the first. Regardless of this consideration, however, once such a basic patriarch-scion relationship becomes established, the progeny's debt, whether direct and real or imagined and historically fortuitous, must be paid. The loyalty of the "discovers" to the "discovered" often then becomes undivided, and we must beware of opening the floodgates to all manner of wishful thinking, embroidery of fact, and pure fabrication germane to the fortunate "foundling." Runge, for one, has already run the full gamut of such smothering devotion.

Thorough scholarship of the Early Romantic Movement in Germany acknowledges the fact that the art and literature of that period can only be understood properly when it is viewed as an intrinsic part of a broader cultural phenomenon, namely, a Christian revival. If we recognize in revivalism with its attendant syndrome of complex psychological currents —currents as varied as the number of individual "religious seekers" who lacked an effective central doctrinal guidance—the antecedent of that period's artistic productions, we will encounter no great difficulties in understanding the seemingly vexing multiplicity of Romantic "schools," genres, styles, and subjects because the basic religiosity of the contents of the works themselves will provide us with the unifying factor. The best efforts of German Romanticism, particularly in its early phases, are directed toward attempts at a rebirth of the Christian spirit. It appears, however, that the initial requirement for the understanding of German Romanticism as an intuitive approach to life based on Christian metaphysics is generally not considered as having necessarily to emanate from a

24

spontaneous apprehension, similar to that which inspired the artists under investigation. The contention is that a rational schema of analysis can be superimposed upon the occult, permitting one thereby to unravel its secrets logically. But the non-sequitur nature of that argument is as patently clear as the mystery of religious faith is obscure. Therefore an understanding of Runge, the most religious of all the Romanticists, cannot be based solely on reasoned logic.

Were Runge's paintings and drawings alone being considered here, we might easily, although against the expressed wishes of the artist, merely employ the requisite critical apparatus reserved for such occasions and, without any emphatic participation in the feelings of the artist, arrive at an "objective and judicious evaluation" of the style and content of Runge's oeuvre. However, we are dealing with his theory, that is, a doctrine which involves not only the new form in art to be created but, above all, the new spirit from which the new form must germinate, a fundamental pedagogical dogma which must be assimilated a priori to the act of apprehension and practice of the "new romantic art"—assimilated intuitively, for, as we have just shown, it cannot be "reasoned out." To understand Runge's intentions, we can be neither wholly objective, nor can we in utter subjectivism (particularly not in the context of a methodical treatise) argue by authoritative proclamation. Neither heated polemics nor pontifical oracles are in order; instead, however, a mixture of sympathy, gentle feelings, intuitive involvement, passionate objectivity and, not least of all, humor.

Runge's artistic theory is anchored in his religious faith. A knowledge of its premises, therefore, cannot be gained by inference but only through instantaneous cognition. An analogy with Jacob Böhme urges itself upon our attention. It is C. J. Barker's opinion, in *Pre-Requisites for the Study of Jacob Böhme*, that the mystic cannot be judged from a philosophical platform that either considers itself to be superior to, or endeavors to explain by means of semantical games, the nature of his mysticism. Neither Böhme's nor Runge's "systems" constitute polemics but rather statements of facts as they happen to exist in their authors' imagination. When Runge says that he believes in angels, (e.g., in his letter to Daniel, Nov. 7, 1802, *H.S.*I, pp. 18–19; in his letter to Gustaf Runge, *H.S.*I, p. 204) we had best believe him, for just as Henri Rousseau's specters ultimately "explain" the wizardry of his neo-primitive compositions, so also do Runge's angels "explain" the magic of his romantic art.

Dresdner expresses the same thoughts regarding general literature on art thus: "One of the great deficiencies in our . . . literature on art is the fact that in many instances it treats the personalities and creations in art with an *icecold sobriety*, in a *pseudo-scientific herbarium style* which is in the case of these things equally as intolerable as it is wrong and fruitless. For art can and must only be comprehended and represented artistically—or else the picture which is given of it becomes a caricature, a blood- and lifeless schema" [italics mine] (*Der Maler der Frühromantik* [*Ph. O. Runge*], p. 2). It would surely appall Dresdner were he to discover that the unfortunate trend which he so deplores has now reached nearly epidemic proportions.

If we can intuit Runge's faith, the feeling for his theory will come automatically. In the more than nine hundred pages of Runge's written testimony there is hardly a single paragraph in which a pious thought, a Bible or catechism quotation is not uttered in conjunction with reflections on art, life, philosophy, music, business, or anything else. Runge says that "to divine God purely in oneself and to feel in one's soul the living breath, is the first thing, and that all things become possible for us through faith and our belief in Him, that we know and can know; but that we must overcome the world and be steadfast in our faith to the end, was taught to us by One, Christ, and he who follows Him must bear the cross upon him" (letter to his brother Gustaf, Sept. 21, 1804, *H.S.*I, p. 203).

Benz observes: ". . . there has hardly ever been an artist in whose letters words from the bible and literal confessions to Christ appear more constantly and in greater abundance than they do in Runge" (*Die Deutsche Romantik*, p. 183). And there is a good reason for that because it was impossible for Runge either to think or act out of context with his faith. His confessional credo was the *terminus a quo* for Runge, he came to it intuitively, and he made it the basis for his life. "I have unconsciously and to me as yet in an incomprehensible manner penetrated, and I could not know, what I do know, if I now should not completely rely on God and on the Gospel of Jesus Christ, because that latter concerns all men in all things and it is the rock and the cornerstone" (letter to his father, Dec. 31, 1802, *H.S.*II, p. 192). Kluckhohn explains this romantic religiosity thus: "That basic impulse of a romantic feeling for life and of a romantic way of thinking, something that we meet again and again, that is the conception for life based on the states of flowing and hovering, of thought in antithesis. These must be overcome in the synthesis and in the higher unity, they urge toward an original foundation, one from which all emanates, and toward a finite unity into which all converges. And with that an essential trait of religious experiencing and of religious longing of Romanticism is already marked. That is a longing for a contact with the Absolute, with God, a longing of the finite to become one with the infinite" (*Das Ideengut der Deutschen Romantik*, p. 131). That, it seems, also is the *conditio sine qua non* underlying Runge's vision of a new art.

Various writers variably ascribe to Runge a fundamentalist persuasion, a Pietist's devotion, an archaic Lutheranism, or see in his mystical

26

excursions into the realm of fantasy Böhmian phantasmagoria, view him as a trans-Alpine convert, a nature mystic, or an all-out pantheist, a Protestant or a Catholic proselyte.

Runge's preference for quoting extended passages from Genesis I and his otherwise candid admission of his belief in biblical history gives us some basis for ascribing to him a fundamentalist faith. Böttcher links Runge's persuasions to the German tradition of Pietism which can be traced back to Jacob Böhme (*Philipp Otto Runge, Sein Leben, Wirken und Schaffen*). Runge's simple unaffected faith in the conduct of daily affairs, his reliance on the catechism, and his frequent quotations therefrom in conjunction with the style of his prose, which is more than usually indebted to biblical phraseology, has caused some writers to christen him an archaic Lutheran. All writers agree that the reading of Jacob Böhme (e.g., *Aurora oder die Morgenröte im Aufgang, Die Drei Prinzipien göttlichen Wesens, Mysterium Magnum*, etc., in *Theosophia Revelata, oder Alle Göttlichen Schriften Jacob Böhmes von Altseidenberg*, 1730) fundamentally shaped Runge's symbolic world view and hence his iconography, his concept of the Trinity as well as his belief in God's revelation in nature and her creative powers.

Runge was decidedly not an atheist (letter to Daniel, Nov. 27, 1802, *H.S.*II, p. 170) nor a Catholic (letter to Pauline, Jan. 13, 1804, *H.S.*II, p. 256), although he deeply felt the power of the Catholic cult of the mass, which helped him in the formulation of his theory of the total work of art or *Gesamtkunstwerk*. (Compare Chapter III for a detailed discussion.) Runge's basic aversion to Catholicism despite some implied neophyte tendencies arising out of the aesthetic experience of the mass is the chief reason for his later estrangement from Tieck, who drifted into the Catholic orbit, as well as the disaffection he felt for the Schlegel brothers and other apologists of the Catholic-inspired Nazarene Movement.

The mystical and pantheistic properties of Runge's complex beliefs will be touched upon throughout this essay. For an excellent, though at times unnecessarily involved and excursive discussion of these and related problems, reference should be made to Otto Georg von Simson's "Philipp Otto Runge and the Mythology of Landscape" (*The Art Bulletin*, XXIV, 1942, 335–350). While it is correct to do so with regard to his art theory, it would of course be erroneous to explain Runge's style and iconography entirely out of religious considerations. We must also take into account his personal "reading" of the history of art and his art critical notions (cf. Chapter III).

What arouses our curiosity and interest even more than the categorization of Runge's confession is the question about the nature of that spiritual force that is released into the world through his belief. "Just as Christ is the Word and the Love which emanated from God, just so the Law is connected with the soul through Him." Runge continues to speak of the

"great love of God to the world" and the need for our uniting in love
". . . so that the Law, i.e. morality and ethics and decency originate in
Love: then and thereby the feeling or the soul is united with the rule or the
body through love." "Love is the Light and the Union of the soul with
matter" (letter to Tieck, April 1803, *H.S.*I, p. 42). The often-stated
parallelism between Runge's idea of love as an active, life-enhancing, and
life-molding force and that of Schleiermacher is really too obvious to
escape anyone's attention (cf. Schleiermacher, *Über die Religion, Reden an
die Gebildeten unter ihren Verächtern*). Runge's concept of love is complicat-
ed by his *Androgynenlehre* derived from Böhme and corresponding *Liebestod* notions (cf. Schmidt, *Philipp Otto Runge*, pp. 76, 130; also Runge's
letter to Besser, April 3, 1803, *H.S.*I, p. 38). It would be straying too far
were we to develop this theme in our context.

A childlike faith, the belief in man as divine tool of God, confidence in
an inspired and constructive synergistic cooperation of man with providence on behalf of the good of the world are Runge's testimony to Protestantism and Romantic Pietism; love is for him that energy through which
alone we can act constructively (letter to Pauline, Weimar, Nov. 15, 1803,
*H.S.*II, p. 246; to his father, Dresden, Jan. 30, 1803, *H.S.*I, p. 31; to a
friend, Hamburg, September 1810, *H.S.*I, p. 213).

Runge told us how to acquire that energy through faith and he tells
us how to maintain its efficacy. "Anyone who does not dare to pour out his
soul into the bosom of another man, will not preserve love. Anyone who
deposits in faith, fidelity and confidence his own innermost self in the
other's soul can only be worthy to receive love in like fashion." With these
words he strikes a chord that is remarkably closely akin to the ideational
leitmotiv of contemporary Existentialist thought. Yet Runge warns: "We
can never say it completely; the complete which we might express would
be the rule or nothingness. In the immediate vicinity of these lies beauty—
anyone who attempts to sustain his life through such perfection will lose it;
anyone who constantly moves closer to it in love and hope and with a pure
conscience, only he will gain it, because he has renounced this life" (letter
to Daniel, July 10, 1803, *H.S.*I, p. 223; letter to Tieck, April 1803, *H.S.*I,
p. 42).

We can see that in Runge's mind notions about ethics and aesthetics
are so finely blended as to appear indeterminable in their respective
spheres. But we can clearly see, nevertheless, that the just quoted "aesthetic
Golden Rule" has the greatest practical importance for the fashioning of
art. Runge says in effect that the means must be regarded as an end in
themselves because perfection in the work itself is forever unattainable.
In the following we will repeatedly encounter statements by Runge which
affirm the supremacy of the act of creation over the final product. That act,
provided it is authenticated by the spirit of piety, sincerity, love, and honest

effort is a creditable end in itself regardless of the finite form it may take.

Runge also believes that the artist must first endeavor to resolve his personal problems in life according to the Christian spirit before he can become an artist in the true sense of the word. The art which follows will then become a series of statements showing outwardly the artist's inner existential conflict with and commitment to life. All these sentiments stand in marked contrast to classical and academic principles and methodology in art which stress, above all, philosophical propriety, literary decorum, and flawless execution in accordance with the tenets and guidelines laid down by the ancients, the old masters, and empirical science. The restrictions on creative freedom imposed by the classical regimen were unbearable impediments to Runge's intuitive approach.

If Runge's statements and pronouncements sound too often vague, ambiguous, vexing, and indeterminate, they do so because in its root Runge's theory of art grows from the humus of an amorphous feeling, an untutored awareness, a naive intuition about the mystery of life rather than from a logically ordered, succinctly organized, systematically comprehended world ideology.

There is much in the makeup of Runge's character and its relation to art that could lend itself to ascribing to him a posture that is commonly referred to as primitivism. Childlike and naïf, pious and sincere, largely untutored, autodidactic, self-reliant, free from all empty gesture and pathos, filled with compassion and love, he sought diligently all his life to give substance to his visionary dreams through a direct, personal, and intimate formal language based largely on the classical formal vocabulary which was best known to him.

The cumulative impression which I received of all his drawings and paintings in the Kunsthalle at Hamburg also contribute in no small measure to my viewing Runge in the light of "primitivism." This circumstance, of course, does in no way diminish but rather tends to increase our problem. Such tendencies as preciousness of execution, exactitude of detail, uncertainty of line, faultiness of anatomy, flatness of space, the additive composition, pronounced symmetry, vertical structural buildup and *horror vacui*, despite many exceptions, impart, in my opinion, to Runge's oeuvre primitivist traits. But because the term "primitivism," beyond providing a convenient label, offers little or nothing in the way of revealing qualitative distinctions over and above the just stated typological generalities regarding style, it is best to leave it at that.

To transform a feeling born of faith and love into an overt, purposive statement of intent, a medium of influence, and process of action, it is necessary to communicate intelligibly. The desire for understanding, fear of misunderstanding, and the need for such a comprehensive language were deeply felt by Runge. Often throughout his letters he says, "I really cannot say the right thing just so, and much less can I write down what I mean," and he expresses through similar statements his communicative difficulties (letter to Tieck, Dec. 1, 1802, *H.S.*I, p. 27). He sought for an intimate language to convey his feelings. "Ever since my childhood I have longed to find words and signs, or something, with which I could make clear to others my inner feeling, namely that which moves calmly and vitally up and down within me during my most beautiful hours" (Dresden, 1801, *H.S.*I, p. 3). Having experienced an ease of communication in the close circle of his own relatives during his childhood, Runge sought the common, direct language of children and the expansion of that personal family unit into a viable world community of kindred souls everywhere, partaking with "hearty joy" in the expression of their feelings in a "family conversation" (Dresden, 1801, *H.S.*I, p. 5). "It would certainly be good to dwell with such a family in which one could thus communicate with one another; and one would have to be a real fool if one were not satisfied and happy with it. Now, it seems to me as if the Apostles, the pious musicians, the great noble poets and painters really had it in mind to form such a family circle" (ibid.).

As to the form of that which we express, Runge goes on to say that we should "at first not be too concerned as to how someone says something but that he really says something and has something to say." Translated for the artist, this statement implies that the desire to create in order to communicate supersedes in importance that which is created. Again, there is an expression of a fluid and dynamic activist aesthetic of participatory involvement to the apparent though presumably provisional or conditional detriment of the work of art. We must take Runge literally at his word when he adds: "Anyone who holds fast within him the beautiful and the good with profound love, he will always reach a beautiful point. We must again become children if we want to reach the best" (*H.S.*I, p. 7). The literal interpretation of the Sermon on the Mount is the only guarantor for the artist to communicate meaningfully with his fellow man without succumbing to the "empty gesture" in his work, according to Runge.

Inasmuch as Runge's practical ethics stand in the closest relationship to his theory of art, his concern with the communication of feelings can only be of vital importance for us. If we were to summarize the content of *Hinterlassene Schriften* in the briefest possible form, we could call them a continuous attempt at communicating his feeling about existence and art; a sustained effort of self-explanation. Although Runge's generation was conversant with the Sturm und Drang literature of the 1770s and its newly discovered intuitivism and therefore did not stand in a position of direct rebellion against the Enlightenment, he nevertheless felt compelled to voice his contempt of that era often, as when he states that the "enlightenment of a human being and the development of his talents must not go further than what his soul can bear" (letter to Daniel, Oct. 16, 1802, *H.S.*II, p. 160).

Concerning formal education he was similarly cautious. He was particularly critical of university study which to him harbored the danger of the destruction of the individual through undigested learning (letter to Brückner, July 9, 1808, *H.S.*I, p. 209). We can indeed state summarily that Runge's whole "body of knowledge" was a feeling, a presentiment. Runge disliked the formulistic or systematic approach to problem solving. He articulates this notion in the following statement which also gives us a clue to the understanding of Runge's whole approach in the arts: "The less someone enjoys and identifies with systems and formulae, the more he understands me. . . . It seems to me that all misunderstanding has come about because science has been taken over by stupidity instead of by wisdom and it is being more and more advertised as wisdom itself" (letter to Daniel, July 1803, *H.S.*II, pp. 222 ff.). Runge seeks the vague presentiment, for the "distinct perception would be the Tree of Knowledge and eating from it causes the Fall of Man." He searches for the natural philosophic cohesion of all creation and experience through synthetic universalizing, for "in that chaos in which most people do not see any coherence, a coherence which itself they consider fantasy, life is already born." He opts for knowledge based on feeling, for "in the soul of man the rays converge, in science they diverge," and as "man loses himself in the immense space, the innocence of feeling with which he started gets lost even as a grain of sand and he thinks himself able to understand the grandeur of creation by destroying himself" (letter to Daniel, April 6, 1803, *H.S.*I, p. 44; to Tieck, April 1803, *H.S.*I, p. 41).

Psychological and nature-philosophical concepts that parallel these Rungian sentiments saw their methodical codification above all in the ideal system of Runge's friend Schelling, and particularly in his *Vom Ich als Prinzip der Philosophie* and *Einleitung zu dem Entwurf eines Systems der Naturphilosophie* (in *Schellings Werke*, Leipzig, 1907). Runge holds out the threat of doom for the future of science. "I believe that we shall have to go through terrible times and if we do not go through them something even more horrible is in store for us, a time when cold creeping reason and intelligence will want to crush the living spark of God." And he warns us against an unscrupulous adherence to principles: "To act purely in consequence of an adopted principle is satanical." Thus Runge sketches in a few brief strokes an accurate prophecy of the satanical horrors of our century (letter to Daniel, July 20, 1803, *H.S.*II, p. 226; cf. Runge's indictment of Goethe's *Faust*, *H.S.*II, pp. 223 ff.; letter to Schelling, Feb. 2, 1810, *H.S.*I, p. 161).

Although Runge dreamed of the innocence of paradise as a state worth emulating, he nevertheless adopted life in a realistic spirit, urged positive action through effort and hard work for civic cooperation in the interest of the community, and despite ill health and hardships he never wavered in his devotion to his family whom he cheered, encouraged, and supported during their worst times (*H.S.*I, pp. 17, 171; *H.S.*II, pp. 250, 328, 332, 335, 348, 360, 376). It would be entirely wrong to classify Runge as a "romantic dreamer" incapable of action (and whatever else that label connotes), and we will see repeatedly later on that he espoused an activist way of life and an art engaged meaningfully in the processes of civic realities.

Runge was a Romantic idealist whose world view was unified by a Pietistic mysticism, a trandscendental nature philosophy and a proto-existentialism grounded in the belief in the life-enhancing force of self-conscious personal activity. "Our life, from non-existence on to the highest existence is only developed to a personality through our own activity" (letter to his father, Feb. 2, 1810, *H.S.*I, p. 182; cf. also his letter to Schelling of Feb. 1, 1810, *H.S.*I, pp. 156 ff. in which Runge discusses Schelling's *Philosophische Untersuchungen über das Wesen der menschlichen Freiheit* which he had just finished reading). Most scholars agree that Existentialism as philosophy germinated with Schelling. His pupil Kierkegaard forms the link with twentieth-century Existentialism. Runge's contribution has not, it seems, received the attention which it deserves. Activity and involvement, genuine feeling, the bona fide "family of man," authenticity of language and communication in the meaningful "dialogue," the miracle of the "I-Thou" relationship in love, all cardinal points of departure for twentieth-century Existentialism—all these ideas germinate in and are unequivocally expressed by Runge! But although he advises one "either to go over to idealism completely and to seek in everything something great, or to take everything in a flat and natural manner," he cautions us against runaway fantasizing when he says that "there is nothing easier and more dangerous than to become absorbed and lost in these ideas and fantasies, so that they never come to an end,—but exactly there are posited their greatness and their beauty" (letters to Daniel, Oct. 16, 1802, *H.S.*I, p. 158; to Daniel, Feb. 13, 1803, *H.S.*I, p. 34; to his father, Dec. 31, 1802, *H.S.*II, p. 191). Does not this demand for a choice ring with the "either-or" contention which Reinhardt considers rightly to be the crux of Kierkegaard's "challenge"? (*The Existentialist Revolt*, pp. 23 ff.; cf. Kierkegaard, *Attack upon Christendom.*)

That categorical alternative between unqualified "complete idealism" and the equally absolute state of the unconditional commonplace, just as Runge's warning of the grave dangers of "fantasizing" as the price we have to pay for "greatness and beauty," may sound contradictory, even irritating to a realist, but such is the strange disposition of Romanticism. Runge's paradoxical nature becomes even more vexing when he warns us "of thinking of the thinking of the thought" and of "hypothesizing from hypotheses" as detrimental to his goals and at another point invites us to "lose ourselves among the most wondrous, lovable and beautiful fantasies, thoughts and occurrences" and to "return into our own peculiarities" in order there "to find in our private inclinations the mirror of those glories." By means of "such efforts we could in the end arrive at a point where we would actually find that mirror if we really go about our seeking in a pure manner" (letter to Daniel, April 6, 1803, *H.S.*I, p. 44; to Dr. Schildener, April 13, 1805, *H.S.*I, p. 196).

Runge's fear of the hypothetical snake biting its hypothetical tail brings to mind Hegel's notion of the Absolute or God and Russell's critique of it, namely, that the Absolute Idea with which the logic of Hegel ends is something like God who is thought thinking about himself, that is, pure thought thinking about pure thought. Russell adds: "That is a professor's God" (*A History of Western Philosophy*, Book III, Part II, Chapter 22, "Romantic Movement, Rosseau, Kant, Hegel," New York, 1946). Parallels with Hegel can again be discerned concerning their respective art historical theorems, specifically the notion of the "death of art." (Compare Chapter II.) What Runge seems to mean with that "mirror" is probably nothing else but Novalis's "Blaue Blume," or the "Stone of Wisdom," as it were. Schlegel in his *116th Fragment* also uses the extended simile of "reflecting mirrors" to circumscribe the infinity of his "progressive-universal" poetic objectives.

Now, Kant demonstrated that we cannot know the "thing in itself." But Runge and the other romantic idealists—despite the former's significant departures from ideal essentialism toward "real" Existentialism—found it impossible to resign themselves to such restrictions on man's genius and freedom. All of Romantic transcendentalist thinking in its endlessly meandering search for the attainment of an ever elusive ideal can in fact be seen as an attempt at proving Kant wrong.

We can perhaps accept in the paradoxical nature of Runge's attitude the very paradox of Romanticism and see in his proclivity for objective analysis (as witness his color theory) on the one hand, and subjective synthesis on the other, the personal Rungian expression of the wider characteristic of German Romanticism as such, which collectively both intuited the universe as an organic oneness born from the idea—thereby giving birth to the soaring structure of transcendental philosophy—and founded the basis of modern scholarship and science in the areas of archeology, linguistics, art history, anthropology, sociology, and other disciplines. The systems of Fichte, Schelling, Steffens, Novalis, Runge, and above all Hegel all have one notion in common—that the world is a construct of the mind. From this can be deduced that Runge's art, being in effect an idea of an idea, that is, standing in a relationship to reality which is twice removed from it, provides no rational basis for its analysis but must be taken at "face value" and on "faith" alone. The same is true of the first three points of his "Ten-Point Program." (Compare Chapter II.)

Runge compares "the highest revelry and passion of the human soul" to "natural phenomena" which we must fathom deeply and accurately, and he goes on to say: "Also, no one who wants to accomplish the extraordinary can be enough of an idealist (not just for fun) and not draw all that lives and exists into his idea of the world and its coherence" [*sic*] (letters to his father, Jan. 13, 1803, *H.S.*I, p. 28; to his brother Gustaf, Sept. 21, 1804, *H.S.*I, p. 201). We shall see later on how Runge proposed to translate that all-inclusive "idea of the world and its coherence" into a new "landscape art" composed of such building blocks, elements, and symbols as connote "all that lives and exists." Runge also sounds a warning not to get lost in ideas completely, to found happiness on civil realities and work and thus sustain one's spiritual integrity through roots anchored in the humus of popular ethos, and above all not to fall prey to sensualism (*H.S.*I, p. 28). Runge, torn between artistic-romantic and bourgeois-realistic affinities, opted for the maintenance of both. His sense of civic responsibility was in no small measure influenced by Schiller (cf. *supra*, pp. 21, 22). Beenken emphasizes the point: "By stressing those elements which the efforts of the artist and the work of a man in a civic profession have in common, Runge overcomes on the human level the most severe narrow-mindedness of the doctrine of genius propounded by the Storm and Stress Movement and of earliest Romanticism" (*Das Neunzehnte Jahrhundert in der Deutschen Kunst*, p. 91). Runge transgresses the limitations of the swooning Storm and Stress era and integrates artistic genius and sensibility with the fabric of civic realities and the attendant—at least qualified —pragmatism necessitated by them.

Thus we see Runge treading a dangerously narrow path that leads him over a calamitous ridge balanced between fantasy and reality, God and earth, threatened at all times by the bottomless precipices of the Seven Sins. And he is very much aware of his dilemma, because he quotes Matthew 7, verses 13 and 14 repeatedly. "Enter by the narrow gate. For wide is the gate and broad is the way . . ." (e.g., *H.S.*I, p. 41). But he also says:

Anyone who does not know it, cannot imagine how unspeakably far revelry and enthusiasm can go in a human being and people use these terms much too loosely. It is the most horrible thing that I know of to become submerged in this vortex, and there is not one among thousands who emerges from it healthy, and yet, anyone who wants to comprehend and grasp the chaos and senselessness of our age, who wants to participate, who wants to return everything to proper limits must go through with it (letter to his father, Dec. 31, 1802, *H.S.*II, p. 192).

It was Novalis who in his *Heinrich von Ofterdingen* gave his fictional hero the task of searching for the Blue Flower which did not exist at all, and thus provided posterity with the most concise and most meaningful metaphor of Romanticism coined to this day. But few were those who self-consciously and intentionally set out in actual life to pursue unto death the search for the Blue Flower. Runge was one of these few. "I shall never set for myself a goal that I can reach, because what would happen to desire, if we saw behind the goal the leftover patch of empty ground!" (letter to Daniel, Nov. 14, 1802, *H.S.*II, p. 164).

It remains for us to determine if Runge's notions concerning faith, love, feeling, education, fantasy, work, society, longing for perfection—in short, his ethics, collectively speaking—have universal human relevancy, if they constitute a meaningful, generally obliging basis for a specific art theory, and if they represent in fact the *conditio sine qua non* of Runge's personal art theory as such. As has been seen so far, the first question is one concerning the universal worth and soundness of the romantic spirit in general and is therefore a "philosophical question." It concerns the pragmatic and the ideal attitudes toward life. Depending upon whether one follows Plato's idealism or Aristotle's scientism one will either embrace romantic idealism as healthy or reject it as sick. Fichte put the problem as a matter of personal choice: idealism sees in things the product of consciousness, whereas dogmatism sees in consciousness the product of things; these two explanations are in total contradiction to each other and he urges one to choose either mode depending "on what sort of man one is." (Compare Windelband, *A History of Philosophy*, p. 580.) I therefore suggest that Goethe's famous expression "Romantisch ist das Kranke, Klassisch ist das Gesunde" is merely an expression of a *Weltgefühl* based precisely on such a personal choice, that is, one which is not founded on faith as the harbinger of knowledge.

If we accept post-Kantian idealism and its metaphysical systems of thought as universally valid constructs—opt for transcendentalism—the second question must necessarily be also answered in the affirmative. With the reservation, of course, that Runge's Romantic art theory in the final analysis cannot be learned but must be intuited and experienced and that that intuition and experience grows out of an individual's religion or life's philosophy. This is, incidentally, also the leading thesis of Kandinsky's art theory in *Das Geistige in der Kunst* and also of Klee's theory in *Pädagogisches Skizzenbuch*. That Romantic art theory or art cannot be "learned" is its most important distinguishing characteristic from classic-academic art, which, according to its leading tenets, can both be taught and learned. Kandinsky says in "Kunstpädagogik," in *Zeitschrift fur Gestaltung* (Dessau, 1928): "Art really cannot be learned. All is intuition-romanticism."

The third question, if not already clearly answered by Runge's own statements so far, may be further examined in the light of his testimony. "I have surely dedicated myself completely to the most pure that is in man, I seek it and I will find it." Runge asserts that he "wants to build an art based on the fundament of all our faith, on our revealed religion" (letters to Böhndel, Nov. 7, 1801, *H.S.*II, p. 96; to Daniel, Nov. 27, 1802, *H.S.*I, p. 21). The art which he will propose must be understood "from the deepest mysticism of religion, because that is where it originates and that must be its solid fundament, otherwise it will collapse as the house built on sand" (letter to Tieck, Dec. 1, 1802, *H.S.*I, p. 27). But art, according to Runge, *is not religion* (cf. *H.S.*II, pp. 174 ff.). "Religion is not art, religion is the highest gift of God, it can only be expressed more magnificently and comprehensively through art" (*H.S.*II, p. 148). Perthes recorded a statement by Runge in which the artist suggests that a poet who has raised art to religion should be "drowned with a millstone around his neck in the ocean where it is deepest" (*Friedrich Perthes' Leben*; cf. *H.S.*II, pp. 105 ff.).

As to what art should try to accomplish, Runge proposes that it must "unlock the most holy for man." Concerning the spirit of the prospective artist he suggests that no man can become an artist if he gambles with the innocence of his soul; he cannot accomplish anything without love, for without the right spirit no art but only handicraft can come about (letter to Clemens Brentano, Dec. 5, 1809, *H.S.*I, p. 188; cf. letters to his father, March 26, 1802, *H.S.*II, p. 121; to Daniel, Oct. 6, 1801, *H.S.*II, p. 92). Runge also admits that he could easily become a theoretical artist, for "even in art there is something that is better than to make works of art" (letter to Daniel, May 11, 1803, *H.S.*II, p. 214).

Beatrix von Ragué in "Das Verhältnis von Kunst und Christentum bei Ph. O. Runge" (unpublished inaugural dissertation, Bonn, 1949) addresses herself to the special problem of Runge's Christianity in relation to his art. She summarizes (pp. 135 ff.) as follows: Runge stressed subjectivity. He searched for a generally comprehensible and universally obliging (*"allgemeinverbindlich"*) art, and he tried to do that with new signs and symbols, a new subjective language. Because, Ragué thinks, this proposition is unfeasible, Runge had to fail. His symbolism, she suggests, did not grow organically but was forced. Runge's art was later not understood in its religious context for lack of an effective symbolic language that would have enabled him to be understood universally. Her thesis is that while Runge's theory and art flowed out of the Christian impulse, yet his work in and by itself cannot be interpreted as having any connection with Christianity.

My discussion of Runge's iconography (Chapter V) substantially corroborates Ragué's findings with the proviso, however, that such an art based on a subjective "open symbolism" (with all its limitations and

LEAVES AND FIRELILY

white silhouette on black background
76×58 cm.
H. K. Inv. No. 2031

CRESS

pen and ink
25.3 × 31.5 cm.
H. K. Inv. No. 1932/139

Nasturtium.

JOHANN DANIEL RUNGE

1799, black and white crayon on brown paper
48 × 36.2 cm.
H. K. Inv. No. 1939/21

THE RETURN OF THE SONS

1800, pen and ink
44.5×63 cm.
H. K. Inv. No. 34128

ACHILLES BATTLING THE RIVER GOD SCAMANDROS
1801, pen and ink and opaque white on brown paper
53×67.2 cm.
H. K. Inv. No. 34231

TRIUMPH OF AMOR

1801/1802, oil on canvas
66×173 cm.
H. K. Inv. No. 2691

ARION'S SEA JOURNEY

1809, pen and ink and watercolors
50.6×118.4 cm.
H. K. Inv. No. 1027

SELF-PORTRAIT

1802/1803, oil on canvas
37.1 × 37.1 cm.
H. K. Inv. No. 1002
loaned to Hamburg Kunsthalle by Dr. Fritz Runge

MORNING

1803, pen and ink
72.1×48.2 cm.
H. K. Inv. No. 34174

EVENING

1803, pen and ink
72.1×48.2 cm.
H. K. Inv. No. 34170

NOON

1803, pen and ink
71.7×48 cm.
H. K. Inv. No. 34177

NIGHT

1803, pen and ink
71.5×48 cm.
H. K. Inv. No. 34181

WIFE OF THE ARTIST IN GREEN DRESS

1804, oil on canvas
72×53 cm.
H. K. Inv. No. 1006

SELF-PORTRAIT IN BLUE COAT

1805, oil on oakwood
39×33 cm.
H. K. Inv. No. 1020

THE SOURCE AND THE POET

1805, pen and ink
50.4×67 cm.
H. K. Inv. No. 34257

THE NIGHTINGALE'S LESSON (Second Version)

1805, oil on canvas
104.7 × 86.5 cm.
H. K. Inv. No. 1009

THE MOTHER AT THE SOURCE

1805 (?), destroyed by fire, oil on canvas
62.5×78.1 cm.
H. K. Inv. No. 1010

licenses) cannot be discounted as an existing and thriving possibility in the twentieth century. Moreover, we must add a further important qualification: Runge's inability to realize empirically the consequences of his theory does not at all arise out of his invention of an unorthodox symbolic imagery which admittedly has nothing or at best very little in common with the conventional body of Christian iconography. (His figurative language as such really merely represents an all too literal visual interpretation of a particular—if minor—strain of mystical phantasms existing in one of Protestantism's variegated confessional subdivisions. As such it can only be considered unchristian if we judge it from a platform of doctrinaire Catholic orthodoxy.)

The reasons for Runge's failure cannot therefore be sought in the motivations which compelled him to work, hence not in Christianity nor in his invention of a new symbolism per se, but rather in the extrinsic hindrances to and the intrinsic limitations of his creative power as an artist which prevented him from fulfilling in practice the full scope of his theory. Thus, it seems, Ragué proceeds from faulty premises to arrive at correct conclusions.

Let us conclude our survey of Runge's general attitudes with the following illuminating statements from *Hinterlassene Schriften*. Runge says

I wish it were not necessary that I carry on with art, because we should go beyond art and it will not be known in eternity. I for my part would not need art if I could live outside the world as a hermit. Art, as it happens to be and has been, is an absurd and learned thing if we look at it as one usually does; but if people looked at the world as children, art would be a pretty language. Therefore, let them speak it who understand art in that way; would not people dance when they hear the music. More than for centuries it is apparent in our age that true art is the only thing which must be sought and it is the one thing which is sought least of all. I have tried to penetrate what t r u e art may be, what an artist must seek to obtain first, what may be the f i r s t b e g i n n i n g o f a w o r k o f a r t. [*sic*]

For Runge the "times urge us toward the theoretical apprehension of all knowledge" in which "thoughts are pursued purely and conscientiously" and in their greatness, so that "in a time where it is possible to do so little as in ours and the power of ideas is so great" they may through the "clarity and bounty" of their effect be more useful in disseminating "concepts about natural forces" than "painting a lot of pictures just to master technique" (letters to Daniel, July 10, 1803, *H.S.*II, p. 223; to Daniel, Oct. 6, 1801, *H.S.*II, p. 87; to Quistorp, June 26, 1807, *H.S.*I, p. 77).

I have already sketched in the briefest possible form Runge's relation to the major formal currents in late eighteenth- and nineteenth-century

German art. While that discussion centered on specific movements and their representative personalities, the following will expand somewhat more on these relationships in general terms, compare German with French art, and also take issue with those cultural currents of the Empire period that have special significance for Runge.

The *philosophes* prepared and the French Revolution executed a radical departure in Western man's relationship to God, one ultimately leading to atheism. German Enlightenment literature and philosophy in large part echoed and expanded upon the French notions which centered in rationalism, humanism, and atheism. Neither France nor Germany, therefore, provided Runge with the proper ideational sounding board for his Pietistic, naïf-intimate religious sentiments, although they did furnish him with certain important concepts, such as ideal ethical doctrines concerning freedom, duty, and civic conduct. (We have seen, for example, that Runge assimilated certain of Schiller's maxims, and we have also pointed out that the regionalist Claudius in his espousal of educational goals based on sincere piety came very close to Runge's own fundamentalist Christianity.) Runge saw in the events of his time as they were reflected or anticipated by contemporary literature and aesthetics a grave threat to his own personal moral and ethical Christian standards in particular and to the cultural future of Europe—as he envisioned it—in general. In stemming this progressive trend toward "moral degeneracy," that is, de-Christianization, Runge recognized the most noble task of a good Christian. Thus, according to Runge, the greatest evil, the decline of the German Christian spirit, had first to be redressed before a new Christian art could even be contemplated by anyone.

Because the "Grand Tradition" of Western art was always inextricably entwined with the Christian religion, a fundamental reshaping of the purposes and goals of art had to follow the cataclysmic cultural upheavals of the French Revolution. Catholic France, in violent opposition to centuries of tutelage to the "sacred establishment" of church and state, found its new expression in the fully secularized, politically tendentious, propagandistic-didactic-classic realism of the art of David and his school. Another main current in France emanated from the Géricault-Delacroix school and an art which espoused a visual translation of literary Romanticism, contextually—that is, was therefore, in the main, narrative-anecdotal —and the Baroque form, stylistically. Both of these two major currents departed significantly from the traditional thematic context in that, generally speaking, neither perpetuated the Christian complex of subjects but instead concentrated in their contents chiefly on pagan myth, secular history, or else significant contemporary events. Conversely, both can be regarded as stylistic progenies of a centuries-old French classic tradition.

Germany was not touched by any effective revolutionary upheavals at the close of the eighteenth century and therefore was not violently led into a new cultural course by a "revolution from below." Hence, unlike France, Germany was not subject to a nationwide aesthetic coordination by the fiat of a popular tyranny—and so continued to direct the artistic expression "from above" and according to variegated aristocratic maxims and standards of long duration.

The artistic over-all picture of Germany during Runge's lifetime, therefore, unlike that of France which easily yields to sensible classification, offers a bewildering array of parallel, overlapping, and opposing trends. Above all, we must count the two major currents of waning Baroque art, namely theatrical illusionism and genre realism. These were especially popular in the Catholic regions of Southern Germany and Austria. Moreover, the playful, gracious, and elegant Rococo style continued everywhere, with slight modification on the norm, especially in portraiture, well into the nineteenth century. Third, we must count the stolid Neoclassicism of the Winckelmann-Mengs School and its many followers. It stood, unlike French Neoclassicism, in no organic formal relationship to past historical styles on native soil. Its capital was Weimar, the Goethe-Kunst-Meyer (Hans Heinrich Meyer) team its chief promoter. Fourth, we must mention the new, Dutch-influenced empirical realism— the beginnings of which can be traced separately in England, France, and Germany—which began to affect landscape artists seriously, especially in the North German and Danish regions. Finally, we cannot overlook the initial stirrings of "romanticism,"—traces of it made up of elements of the spiritual, mysterious, visionary, otherworldly, dreaming, haunting, unfulfilled, yearning, and restless which affected the thematic dispositions if not the styles and techniques of certain artists regardless of their formal affiliations. Thus Runge was born into an era which was both stylistically pluralistic, even chaotic, and thematically incompatible with his peculiarly individualistic ideas regarding the technique, style, and content of a new Christian art, an art based on a personal experiencing of God in his revelation. He had no models to follow.

The problem of elucidating German artistic trends during Runge's lifetime also requires other clarifications. While French Classicism and Romanticism in art were, in all their various phases, essentially rational, nonproblematical, and nonspeculative, although as a rule highly "idealistic," both German Classicism and Romanticism in art were in addition to being "idealistic" also problematical, speculative, and irrational. (Only Delacroix at times comes close to the Germanic complexity of feeling.) Attempts at establishing a marked distinction between German Classicism and German Romanticism are really quite futile. There can be no question, of course, that that typically German trend was enhanced, corroborated, and supported by German Romantic literature and philosophy, particularly by the Jena School which professed a transcendental or absolute idealism with a host of attendant fantasies and concomitant chimeras. Runge stood in very close contact to both Romantic literature and philosophy. Therefore, Runge was heir to and combined in his attitude, in addition to given tenets of Enlightenment ethics, both idealism and Germanic speculative meditation in the crucible of his passionately confessed Lutheranism. Being a child of his times, Runge adopted the formal language which seemed to be best suited for that Germanic idealism, namely the classical formal vocabulary, while incorporating into it all such "romantically" meditative ideas as were analogous to his moral, ethical, Christian, and mystical stirrings. He thereby taxed Classicism's "formal" tolerance for thematic adaptability beyond its capacity. This also explains the curiously hybrid character of Runge's own style.

Another consideration requiring our attention arises out of Runge's approach to the above "formula" of a new ideal, Classical, Romantic, Christian art. That is his insistence (to be discussed at length further on) on building the new art on the solid foundation of empirical science and the exact observation and measurement of natural phenomena, particularly of color. But unlike other realists and naturalists who considered the reproduction of the natural form as an end in itself, Runge merely regarded it as a means to an end, a necessary first step toward the attainment of infinitely more complex goals. Thus the "dualistic" ideal-classical and utopian-romantic merge imperceptively and become entwined in Runge's theory not only with each other but also with the "monolithic" empirical-scientific-realistic-naturalistic aesthetic concepts.

The terms "dualistic" (*dualistisch*) and "monolithic" (*monolistisch*) derive from Rudolf Zeitler's dissertation *Klassizismus und Utopia* (1954). Here he groups Romanticism and Classicism, as generically indistinguishable from each other and as moving simultaneously toward the real and the ideal, into the first category and the unequivocally pragmatically directed Realism of mid-nineteenth-century France, including Impressionism, into the second. I believe that Zeitler's unorthodox and controversial categorization is excellent and will go a long way toward discontinuing the unfruitful debate about "differences" between Romanticism, Classicism, and Realism. Zeitler's expanded views on the topic have become available to the general public in his *Geschichte der Kunst des Neunzehnten Jahrhunderts* (1967). Only if we adopt a concordant premise that recognizes the confluence of Classicism, Romanticism, and Realism with their attendant ideational and stylistic doctrines in Runge's ultimate plan, can we understand his theories in all their sweeping consequences. It can be seen that Runge endeavored to encompass nearly the full scope of all available possibilities of artistic expression and to fuse them into a unified theory.

We must at this point be reminded that Runge's pioneering of a new art movement is concerned with visual and not literary maxims and criteria. Swiss nature lyricism, Klopstock's religio-epical "Miltonism," Herder's irrational "Rousseauism," and Goethe's Wertherian hyper-emotionalism had broken violently with the Gellertian modes of pseudo-classicism, thereby ushering in some of the important prerequisites of a later and thoroughgoing literary revolution by such of Runge's friends and contemporaries as, for example, Wackenroder, Tieck, Novalis, and F. Schlegel. However, no such bases of departure were laid for Runge prior to his time in art. The name of Carstens comes to mind at once in this context. But regardless of some unconvincing arguments to the contrary, the Neoclassicist Carstens belonged to an "older generation to an older century" (cf. Pauli, *Philipp Otto Runge's Zeichnungen*, p. 13).

Conversely, Carus, who worked in at least partial analogy to Runge's ideas about landscape, belonged to a younger generation, could therefore not have been a medium of influence on Runge. (We shall touch upon Carus's theories concerning landscape art later on.)

Runge's contemporary Fuseli (who may have been known to Runge because of his international reputation) must be discounted as an "influence." Fuseli's individualistic, "Gothic" horror art stands in the same diametrical opposition to Runge's objectives, as stand, for example, E. T. A. Hoffmann's tales to those of Eichendorff.

The "influence" of Blake on Runge's art is at best a very problematical issue. The most recent state of the problem tends to discount the influence of Blake's highly subjective language on Runge fairly completely (cf. Berefelt, *Philipp Otto Runge*, pp. 164 ff.; S. Waetzold, "Philipp Otto Runges 'Vier Zeiten'" inaugural dissertation, Hamburg, 1951, pp. 66 ff.). Discussions of similarities between the two artists' theories must be viewed as polemical disputations attempting to link parallel and independent developments. Runge's relationship as artist-theorist to his friend C. D. Friedrich—a vexing problem—will be discussed repeatedly later on, especially in Chapters III and V.

Faced with a generally acknowledged breakdown and corruption of the once viable late Baroque and Rococo art into what appeared to him empty form and meaningless gesture and a seeming lack of ethical purpose of artistic trends in general, confronted with the discrediting of the Christian religion, a process gaining rapidly in momentum and thereby threatening with obliteration the very raison d'être of the "Grand Tradition" of occidental art, Runge was left to his own resources and conscience which urged upon him the necessity of a spiritual regeneration of humanity first, before a new art form could even be contemplated by anyone. Runge called for nothing less than a Renaissance affecting all men spiritually and morally and therefore aesthetically. Neither the antiquarianism and eclecticism which originated with Winckelmann, the champion

II. MANIFESTO

*T*HE year 1802 of Runge's Dresden period, as has been noted, had far-reaching consequences for his life, the most important development in our context being, of course, the formulation of his so-called Ten-Point Program, or as I shall call it, perhaps more succinctly, his "Manifesto." It is contained in a letter to Daniel from Dresden and dated March 9, 1802 (*H.S.*I, pp. 7 ff.). Runge does not call the part of his theory presently under discussion a "program" nor does he entitle it by any other heading. It is significant to note (also as an apologia for this study) that one of the most perceptive and illuminating critics of Runge, G. Berefelt, felt it necessary to state the following as late as 1962: "It seems to me that Runge's biographers have neither payed sufficient attention to the scope of the artist's purely theoretical endeavors, nor to the basic implication of his formative theories. With the passage of time his preoccupation with theory became increasingly more predominant" (*Bemerkungen zu Ph.O. Runges Gestaltungstheorie*, p. 51). At least two reasons might be advanced for this oversight. First, the considerably greater interest professed by scholars in Runge's practical oeuvre stimulated, no doubt, by the unquestionable challenge the works themselves pose to the critical acumen of anyone who has come into direct contact with them. Second, the disorganized and informal manner in which Runge's theories appear in his *Hinterlassene Schriften*, a compendium of the artist's letters over a period of about ten years.

Thus, it seems, the task of isolating and ordering the significant from casual observations and extraneous reports represents an obstacle formidable enough to have discouraged most scholars. This so-called Manifesto, however, represents the rare incidence of a sequential, declaratory exposition of Runge's artistic program in logical progression and sustained over nine pages in *Hinterlassene Schriften*, in which he thinks through his entire process of artistic creation from initial intuition to the final brushstroke on the canvas. Runge proceeds here step by step to move from a supramundane, transcendental experiencing of the living presence of God to the terrestrial spheres of the ontic immanency of the material product of the artist.

It cannot be emphasized sufficiently strongly that the intrinsic logic of Runge's train of thought throughout his "Manifesto" must be left intact, taken at face value, and not be subjected to extrinsic polemics or else it will crumble to dust. We cannot judge Runge (as with most of Romanticism's ideas) from a lofty and philosophical platform because, after all, he did not address himself to philosophers and scholars but to ordinary men and artists. Therefore the Rungian doctrine should be understood more in the light of pedagogy and studio instruction, a situation then which requires the unreserved surrender of one's own prejudices to the letter and spirit of the method—which may be authoritative with or without adequate grounds—rather than in the light of aesthetics as a branch of philosophy.

If we therefore recognize that we should not deal with Runge's theory as though it were a logically based and conclusively verifiable philosophical system and hence the proper target for academic sophistry (as is all too often done in the case of Runge) but rather act as though we were Christian artists in search of an appropriate avenue of approach to our profession and abandon ourselves in our thoughts to an imagined classroom situation—in short, if we accept the "method" for what it is as if in a pedagogical experiment—then we will come much closer to recognizing Runge's theory in its true and Rungian spirit than would be possible by any other means. This approach will also show us that Runge, had he chosen as his profession theology instead of art, would undoubtedly have elected dogmatics as his "field of specialization."

We may also speculate about the eventual productions of the "Runge School" had it ever established itself. Can we assume that it might have, as other schools before and after Runge, deteriorated into a "tyranny of form and style" once these were codified as "classic"? Or can we assume that, having been built on the ideational basis of the ultimate human concern, namely, the belief in the Triune God and his covenant with the faithful, and having as its goal the glorification of that faith, it would have opened the floodgates of maximum self-expression for the duration of that belief's period of temporal vitality and human relevancy? Surely the latter must be supposed if we disregard the actual historical development of Christianity in the nineteenth century and that process of disintegration which Runge considered the most noble task of man to overcome, and of course also if we choose to opt for the "legitimacy" of the Christian religion in our modern age, in the first place. But regardless of all that, we must resign ourselves to the "facts of life" which simply do not provide for the Parousia to be set in motion by a handful of artists, no matter how devoted they may be to their calling. Since the rest of Runge's thought throughout

44

his endless writings constitutes, in effect, supporting arguments for, explanations of, and enlargements upon the "Manifesto," it seems best to devote this chapter almost entirely to the discussion of the "Manifesto" of March 9, 1802.

Runge had already during his first stay in Hamburg eagerly sought to establish a spiritual contact with contemporary Romantic literature, philosophy, and art theory, and had left the Copenhagen academy out of protest, in large part, against the Neoclassical teaching methods there. However, although prior to his arrival in Dresden he was fully preconditioned to overthrow the whole Neoclassical art program, the actual overt reaction was triggered by his failure in the Weimar art competition (compare Chapter I).

It is advisable here to summarize briefly exactly that which Runge chose to oppose, namely Goethe's classical program. Goethe's essay *Laokoon*, which follows in its predilection for that theme the *Laokoon oder über die Grenzen der Malerei und Poesie* by Lessing, contains in a nutshell Goethe's theory concerning what he calls "truth and probability" in works of art. Whereas the classicist Lessing sets up the limitations of a work of art with respect to the chronological unwinding of events (art being able to show merely a moment of a specific action, an epic poem, conversely, embracing the temporal development of a continuous event), Goethe differentiates two essential demands in *Laokoon*: the demand of nature, the more important by the way, and the demand of antiquity.

Concerning nature, Goethe further elaborates that one can only see things as they really are if one knows them. Man is the highest and the real object of art. He further reflects upon the necessity of a general color theory for the reproduction of the color effects in nature. He warns against slavish reproduction of nature in all its details, however. He says that nature is only perfect in its entirety. One should never paint a being but the idea of the being. Furthermore, art should satisfy both the intellect and the emotions. The "characteristic" work of art must also undergo a "heightening" or intensification in order to speak also to the emotions. The "characteristic," on the one hand, and the intensification on the other, however, are not sufficient. In addition, "beauty" must be introduced. The special "truth" of a work of art is born from its own inner consequence, which stands in contrast to the natural realism of, say, a wax replica.

Concerning antiquity, Goethe elaborates further by saying that even as his journal is called *Propyläen*, so also must the artist arrive at the true or antique art through the forecourts. For the Greeks, he continues, perfection was natural, but we wish to attain perfection yet do not achieve this goal. Goethe maintains that it is almost impossible for the German and Northern artist to transgress the boundary which lies between the formless and the form (cf. Goethe, "Laokoon" in *Schriften zur Kunst*, Zürich, 1954).

In an unusually vehement letter in which he vents his pent-up misgivings and wrath against the Weimar and Goethean program, Runge says: "Don't be angry with me because I have gotten too violent, but I assure you Goethe has nearly brought me to the edge of the abyss with all that damned stuff, and what has saved me is that in which he does not believe. I am really mad at him. To put on such airs with such pretensions—and his whole strength lies in his beak!" (letter to Daniel, Dec. 14, 1802, *H.S.*II, p. 173). It should be added in this context, and in anticipation of Chapter III, that Goethe's opinion on the notion of the fusion of the different arts encountered the most outspoken resistance in Runge. Whereas Runge saw in the hybrid total work of art or *Gesamtkunstwerk* the culmination of his highest aims, Goethe condemned such practices as indicative of the decline of art historically and of the degeneration of the individual arts for his own time, in particular.

Just prior to March 9, 1802, in a letter that might be considered a prologue to the "Manifesto," Runge says that the "art competition in Weimar and the whole procedure there is taking altogether a completely wrong direction, one by which it is impossible to effect anything good." At the same time, Runge thus counters Goethe's insistence on the emulation of the classic Greek prototypal form and the spirit of equipoise which engendered it as the prime requisites of modern art: "We are no longer Greeks, we cannot anymore grasp the totality when we view their perfect works of art. Much less can we produce such works. Then why even try to deliver something mediocre? . . . how can we stumble upon such an unhappy idea as to want to recall the old art?" (letter from Dresden, February 1802, *H.S.*I, pp. 5 ff.). It would be well to remember that Wackenroder, who, as has been shown, was a source of influence on Runge, had unequivocally stated his views on the imitation of art at an earlier time. The following statement expresses concisely the writer's sentiments concerning medieval art: "Why don't you condemn the Indian because he speaks Indian rather than our language? And yet you condemn the Middle Ages because they did not build temples as they did in Greece." (Compare "Herzensergiessungen eines kunstliebenden Klosterbruders" in *Deutsche Literatur*, Sammlung literarischer Kunst und Kulturdenkmäler in Entwicklungsreihen, Reihe Romantik, Leipzig: Ph. Reclam Jr., 1931, p. 48.) Thus Wackenroder defends the medieval or perhaps Gothic style against the advocates of the Greek style. The ethnic-nationalist argument was a favorite one with the Romanticists. But Runge used it less than most of them.

Further on in the Dresden letter of February, Runge goes on to speak about the history of art up to his time (cf. Chapter III), the new landscape as he sees it (cf. Chapter V), the divination of a work of art "at the moment" when he "perceives the coherence of the universe," and concludes by saying: "I want to depict my life in a series of works of art; when the sun sinks and the moon gilds the clouds, I want to hold fast the fleeting spirits."

It might be well to consider at this point Runge's attitudes toward travel abroad, specifically, of course, to such artistic centers as Italy and France, and the influence on an artist that would inevitably result from a firsthand knowledge of the Old Masters. His views on that subject seem to have changed considerably during the course of time. In a letter to Daniel (*H.S.*II, p. 93, Oct. 6, 1801) Runge writes: "I wish with all my heart to see a lot of Raphael in France and Italy." As far as actually residing abroad is concerned, however, Runge immediately qualifies his statement by saying that "it is easier to be active in a locality where no real opinions in art dominate." That would, it seems, fairly exclude both of the countries mentioned by him with regard to the relative ease of artistic activities in the Rungian definition of the word. A much more unequivocal statement on the subject of foreign influences can be found in an apparently later but undated letter to Pauline (*H.S.*II, p. 179). After outlining for his bride his plans to bring into being a new art, Runge observes: "Because I want to bring this about, I am convinced that it is necessary that I do not first see Italy and France with regard to great works of art because these will only distract me for a period of time from my idea and suffocate that which at the present stands alive in my imagination."

From these statements, along with Runge's feelings about the art of the ancients, a picture emerges that tends to corroborate Ebstein's thesis (*Tuberkulose als Schicksal*, p. 33) of the unconscious haste of work habits resulting from a premonition of early death, characterizing those afflicted with tuberculosis. It seems that Runge, while admiring certain of these masters, for example, Raphael and Reni, among the "moderns," was at the same time also compelled to hurry on with the task of completing his personal plans in art. In this conflict of priorities the Goethean approach, centering in a comprehensive study of Mediterranean culture, the Renaissance, and the classical Graeco-Roman heritage as a necessary prerequisite for the practice of contemporary art, had quite clearly to lose out to Runge's own subconscious urgings on the brevity of his life which compelled him to hurry on toward his goal without such lengthy preparation. Thus, time was an element so precious in Runge's life as to outweigh in importance even his love for the "great works of art."

In an important first draft for a letter to Schelling eight years later, Runge makes the following explanatory remark concerning the romantic attitude of the artist. The statement seems to summarize the older Runge's general philosophy of art most concisely of all. The meaning of the statement has lost nothing of its validity and power to this day:

The study of the ancients and the development of all the stages of art from it is quite all right. But it cannot help the artist at all if he does not arrive at, or is not brought to view *the present moment of his existence with all its pains and pleasures*; [italics mine] if all that which he meets does not come into personal touch with the widest distance and the most inner core of his existence, with the most ancient past and the most magnificent future. This must not destroy him but must contribute to forming him ever more perfectly. This is, I think, only the general state of the genuine artistic spirit, but in it all things which he uses and needs must dissolve and become transfigured. The world of the Titans exists just as much in the relationship of the angles and figures, as it does in a picture which proceeds out of the general tone through the impasto of the vigorous effect and from the action of the physiognomies and the movement, all of which the artist has to add to the most joyous apparition of the pure moment (letter to Schelling, Feb. 1, 1810, *H.S.*I, p. 160).

Thus Runge, while departing from Neoclassical, antiquarian-esoteric doctrines, enriches art dramatically by relating it meaningfully to the psychological exigencies of the present moment in the life of the artist and by bringing it into the mainstream of contemporary life, for better or for worse.

The "Manifesto" begins with a preamble in which Runge dismisses pat aesthetic formulae such as, for example, "a work of art is eternal" or "a work of art requires the whole man," and more such "phrases" as he calls them and adds that "for some time now a real light had appeared" in his soul which had made him realize everything spontaneously. The subsequent paragraphs treat of Böhmian mystical polarities, for example, of the universal adversaries who, as "granite" and "water" and as "good and evil" are locked in perpetual opposition and combat. (In the context of our discussion the treatment of Runge's purely mystical digressions will be reduced to a minimum.) Runge then goes on to speak of a conversation he had with Tieck in which the latter spoke of the "rise and fall of cultures," the dynamic-cyclical nature of history, and the dramatic polarities resulting from the successively oppositional epochs in the history of art.

The First Point of the "Ten-Point Program" concerns "our presentiment of God" or the "consciousness of ourselves and our eternity" and begins with a romantic-poetic effusion which I count among the most stirring and emotive passages in German literature:

When the sky above me abounds with countless stars, when the wind rushes through the wide space and the wave breaks roaring in the far night, when above the woods the sky turns red; the valley steams and I fling myself upon the grass under the glittering drops of dew, each leaf and each blade of grass teems with life, the earth lives and stirs beneath me, all resounds together in a single chord, then the soul jubilates aloud and soars into the boundless space around me, and

48

there is no below and no above, no time, no beginning and no end, I hear and feel the living breath of God who holds and carries the world, in whom all lives and works: here is the highest that we divine—God!

Runge concludes the passage by saying: "This deepest divination that God is above us, this living soul within us which derives from Him and returns to Him, this is the surest and most distinct consciousness of ourselves and our own eternity." This writer may be forgiven for not being a poet and therefore only able to render a "pedestrian" translation of Runge's inspiring prose.

This prefatory Point One is followed by Point Two, or the "perception of ourselves in connection with the whole" and a discourse on the dynamic-organic-psychological progression of nature, referrals to Böhmian imagery, soaring tropological equations of universal and individual properties of being, parallelisms between art and inanimate objects, nature history and human psychological developments, and by mystical digressions on mother love as being eternally locked in celestial combat with fate. Runge concludes: "This eternal change of things we feel within us, in the whole world, in each inanimate object and in art."

The Böhmian kinetic-progressive-organic view of nature is shared in equal measure by Novalis, Wackenroder, Tieck, Steffens, Schelling, and Runge. The temptation is great of falling into the trap of "rumination" on this and related points. I intentionally leave out most of the mystical-nature-philosophical or nature-scientific material in order to glean the essential from the totally occult. What is important is the spirit of Böhme which makes all things possible to the imagination. The peculiarities of Böhme's system, that is, his numbers theory, alchemistic phraseology, his astrological nomenclature, and so forth, and their adaptations by the romanticists, including Runge, are not essential in our context. May Runge's suggestion of that mystical feeling suffice: "We feel that something relentlessly strict and terribly eternal is locked in the most violent battle with a sweet and infinite love, as something hard and soft, as rocks and water. The rougher this opposition becomes the farther away each thing departs from perfection and the more they unite the closer each thing comes to its perfection" (*H.S.*I, p. 10). However, the arbitrariness of the overflowing feeling, according to Runge, must be bridled into the universal common mold of meaningful symbols, thereby guaranteeing the expression of feeling through existing symbols.

Runge concludes thus:

When our feelings move us to the point when all our senses shake in their fundaments, then we seek for the solid, important signs which were found by others, and we unite them with our feeling. At the most beautiful moment we can communicate it to others. If we try to expand this moment an overstraining occurs,

49

that is to say, the spirit escapes from the signs which we have found and we cannot recapture the coherence within us until we return to the first heartiness of feeling or until we become children again. This circle, where one always dies once, everyone has experienced, and the more often one experiences it, the deeper and more heartfelt the feeling surely becomes. And in that way art comes and goes, and there remains nothing but dead signs, when the spirit has returned to God.

Point Three, or "religion and art" begins, as did Point One, with a poetic effusion:

The feeling of the coherence of the whole universe with us; this jubilating enchantment of the most heartfelt living spirit of our soul; this united chord which in its vibrations touches every string of our heart; the love which keeps us and carries us through life, this sweet being next to us that lives in us and in whose love glows our soul: all these push and press within our bosom, to let us know, we hold fast the highest points of these feelings and thereby are created certain thoughts within us.

The thoughts which come about in this manner, Runge continues, we express in "words, tones and pictures" but the "truth of the feeling possesses everyone," and all therefore praise the one God, and thus comes about that which we call religion. Runge seems to equate the motivations for heathen art with that of Christian art when he speaks of the "symbols of our thoughts concerning the powers of the world, those symbols which are the pictures of God or of the gods," although it is more probable that he may also speak of religious feeling as such. *Bilder* ("pictures") in German and in this context could mean both pictures as well as ideas or notions.

At Point Three, as we have seen, occurs a bifurcation: our feeling of God (Point One) and our feeling of universal coherence (Point Two) collectively give rise to symbols which are used in religion (and in the forming of pictures or "mental pictures" or ideas of God) as well as in art (art being a natural concomitant of religion, as is, incidentally, historically quite true). Runge goes on to say:

We use these symbols when we want to make clear to others great occurrences, beautiful thoughts about nature and the lovely or terrible perceptions of our soul, about events or about the inner coherence of our feeling. We seek for an event or occurence [Runge uses *Begebenheit* which means both] which coincides characteristically with the perception that we want to express, and when we have found it we have chosen the s u b j e c t of art. [*sic*]

The subject of art is Point Four. It was, above all, the absurdity of the proposing of subjects to the entrants of the Weimar art competition that irritated Runge most of all. He saw in the personal choice of the subject by the artist the most essential prerequisite of a work of art. Point Four effects that intimate relationship between subject, content, and feeling of the artist at the present moment of his existence which is the crux of the intuited, personal, subjective, romantic art and that point at which it deviates from reasoned, universal, objective, classical art most decisively, regardless of the many—especially stylistic—similarities between the two. It is to be noted, however, that Runge did not conceive of a communicational difficulty in the personal symbols of which he speaks, but that he considered them, by virtue of their common origin in identical human feelings, even as a readymade "family language." It can therefore be said that while Runge's means were subjective, the ends which he sought were precisely the opposite, namely the generally comprehensible, objectively perceivable, universal, "catholic" art. It is best to continue from here on with the direct quotation of the text to the end, so that the reader may not be led astray by my attempts to present the material in more "concise" or "abridged" form, which is exactly what Runge intended to do in the first place.

Point Five:

By correlating this subject with out perception, we dispose of those symbols of natural forces, or of the feelings within us, against each other, so that they work characteristically for t h e m s e l v e s , for the s u b j e c t and for our p e r c e p t i o n : that is the c o m p o s i t i o n . [*sic*]

Point Six:

Even as we perceive the forms of beings, from which our symbols are taken, more clearly and coherently, so we also derive their contours and representation characteristically from their basic existence [*Grundexistenz*], from our perception and from the makeup [*Consistenz*] of the natural subject. We observe this natural subject in all positions, directions and expressions, we arrange each subject of the whole composition exactly according to nature and in conformity with the composition, [with] the effect, [with] its individual action as such, and [with] the action of the whole work, we let each subject become smaller or larger according to perspective and we observe all accessory matters [*Nebensachen*] and other things that also belong to the fundament in which all is operative, likewise exactly after nature and according to the subject, and that in sum amounts to the drawing.

(The term "design" used in Elizabeth Holt's translation is perhaps too broad in that it does not, properly speaking, and in the designation's common usage, include the fine points of perspective and accessory matters.)

The importance which Runge attaches to color becomes apparent when we observe that Points Seven through Ten deal exclusively with color. Point Seven:

Just as we observe the colors of the sky and earth, the change of colors on people during periods of excitement and perception, as well as in those effects as occur during great natural phenomena, and as we dispose of these colors harmoniously and according to their symbolical values, so in the same manner we give each subject of the composition in harmony with our deepest perception and in harmony with the symbols and subjects as such its proper color, and that process is the disposition of color.

(*"Farbengebung,"* the word Runge uses, may also more aptly be translated as local color or more precisely, the disposition of local color.)

Point Eight:

This we diminish or heighten with respect to its purity, depending upon whether an object should appear closer or farther, or whether the air space between the object and the eye is larger or smaller: that is atmospheric perspective.

(*"Haltung"* meaning bearing, deportment, attitude is, I believe, best translated as atmospheric or aerial perspective in this context.)

Point Nine:

We observe both the consistency of each object in its color from within, as well as the effect of lighter or weaker light upon it, and also the shadow, also the effect of the illuminated object standing next to it upon it: that is the color value [*Colorit*].

Point Ten:

We seek in the reflections and the effects of one object upon the other, and the colors of the latter, for transitions, we observe all colors in harmony with the effect of the air and the time of the day which is taking place, we seek to observe this tone, the last reminiscence [*Anklang*] of the perception, from the ground up, and that is the tone—and the end.

Tone refers to color unity or over-all tonal cohesion or value; Runge distinguishes, in Point Nine, the value of individual objects from the value of the whole picture, in Point Ten. The latter should not, however, be confused with such technical artificialities as, for example, *morbidezza, sfumato, sfumatezza,* or *"Correggiosity."*

At the end of the "Manifesto," Runge summarizes as follows:

Thus art is then the most beautiful endeavor if it emanates from that which belongs to all and is one with it. Here I want once again to enumerate all the prerequisites of a work of art as they follow each other not only with regard to their importance, but also with respect to the succession in which they should be developed:

(1) Our presentiment of God; (2) the perception of ourselves in connection with the whole, (3) religion and art; that is to express our highest feelings through words, tones or pictures; and here then visual art seeks first: (4) the subject; then (5) the composition, (6) the drawing, (7) the disposition of local

color [*Farbengebung*], (8) aerial perspective [*Haltung*], (9) color value [*Colorit*], (10) tone [*Ton*].

We note the stress which Runge places upon the idea of an art that is based on commonly shared feelings; that is, he links art to the commonwealth of humanity, thus proposing to make it, after centuries of estrangement from the people at large, again meaningful to the masses. Paul Klee's famous dictum "Uns trägt kein Volk" ("No people [or nation] supports us") was shared by Runge, and he applied himself to the proposition of redressing that evil. Runge adds the following to his summary:

It is my opinion that no work of art can be created if the artist does not proceed from the first points, no work of art can be eternal otherwise. A work of art which proceeds from these first points and only arrives at the composition in its execution is worth more than all the artificial art which derives from the composition without the preceding tenets, even if it is completed to the tone. It must derive from the inner core of man, otherwise art is play. In Raphael, Michelangelo, Guido, and several others, art germinates in that inner core. Afterwards, they say, art declined. Would that mean anything else but that the spirit has fled? Annibale Carracci, etc., started only with the composition, and Mengs with the drawing; our present noise-makers are only concerned with tone.

(For a summary restatement of the "Ten-Point Program" compare Runge's letter to Böhndel, April 7, 1802, *H.S.*II, pp. 123 ff.)

We see in this statement that Runge attaches the primal importance to the spirit in which an artist works rather than to the degree of perfection he may achieve in his art, particularly when he may be motivated by less than noble aspirations. Runge thus not only breaks away from the conventional academic norm regarding artistic objectives but also lays the ground for a typically twentieth-century sentiment, namely, that which enshrines the attempted, implied, sketched, incomplete, detached, disjointed, and partial work of art in what might best be termed "aesthetics of the discursive and fragmentary." In that way Runge pioneered in art as F. Schlegel did in literature: it is only possible to defend the latter's now celebrated *Lucinde* as a uniquely novel and interesting venture in literature on the basis of that contemporary critical approach and none other.

It may be said that, barring semantical difficulties, points Five through Ten do not pose any problems. Concerning points One through Four, we must trustingly believe in what Runge says, because no critic has as yet succeeded in unravelling lucidly Runge's precepts. Conversely, even as these precepts are built on feeling alone, so also must we perceive them intuitively and without reservations based on scholarly judiciousness. The originality of Runge does not lie in the "invention" of those individual points (nor in their elaboration) which make up his "Manifesto," for each point by itself has been dealt with prior to Runge, and perhaps more successfully by others (e.g., the mystical perception of God by Böhme, Spener, Francke, Zinzendorf, etc., the syncretistic animism by Novalis and Tieck; the unified transcendental nature philosophy by Schelling, Steffens, Baader, Ritter, etc.). Rather, it seems that the importance of the "Manifesto" lies in its combining for the first time all these notions into a unified totality. More important, it focuses that unified world view upon art, thereby providing art with a radically new point of departure, the individual steps of which are articulated in detail; that new point of departure is the romantic premise in art and as such it cannot be rationalized. Runge sees the roots and the origin of art in the unfathomable soul of man. He claims that without the purest and most sincere belief in God, in ourselves, and in others nothing beautiful can be created in this world. This belief in ourselves and others also means the belief in the divine in man and the living force which created Heaven and Earth in the soul of man. The image of this living force must stir in us as the real dynamic energy in the creation of art. There must be love in us and around us. Love and art must be most intimately connected with each other, for the latter is impossible without the former.

In an interesting statement from an essay that was originally intended as an introduction to his color theory (*H.S.*I, pp. 73 ff.), Runge related feeling to the creative impulse, nature to the work of art, while incorporating in part both Goethe's notion of "intensification" (above, p. 45) and Schelling's notion of "creative imagination" (cf. "Transcendental Idealism," *Schellings Werke*), as producing consciously what nature produces unconsciously:

The living coherence of a pure work of art is born directly from the overflowing richness of feeling. The work of art, however, derives its completion from a reflection of the coherence of the exterior form with the most inner emotion. If then, feeling and reflection in a work of art permeate each other most intimately, it will stir the crude man, the dilettante and the artist, each in his own way. The person who produces out of his spiritual and loving urge and has looked into the living force of his soul with a skilled eye, steps before such a perfect work of art with the profound feeling which is stirred with the enchantment of the creation of his own spirit, and if he seriously comprehends the idea and the completion, the production and the reflection, recognizes the coherence of this work with nature, within himself, the whole magnificence of his creation will appear to him as a means to express himself more comprehensively in relation to what he perceives from within and from without. And only that person will really be able to found art anew who recognizes the most beautiful works of art of the past as heightened nature products [*potenzierte Naturprodukte*].

Runge believes that art which is no longer an inseparable "one" with our religion must decline and sink, equally in individual human beings as in entire generations. (That latter concern or Runge's interpretation of the course of the history of art will be discussed in Chapter III.) All along Runge presupposes, as a matter of course, the necessary artistic talent which must underlie all other considerations. In addition, Runge distinguishes between ecstasy (or the emotional experience as such) and the reflective experiencing of that ecstasy which alone, in the crucible of the creative person, can shape the artistic image.

We have previously seen that Runge conceived of the "thinking of the thinking of the thought" as a puzzling idea. Now he shifts from the rational to the irrational-intuitive function by suggesting the notion of the feeling of the feeling of that which is felt. Dresdner thinks that Runge was different from the other early romanticists because, first, he did not participate in psychological experimentation (which often incapacitated the others in a vicious cycle) and, second, because he lacked "romantic irony" (*Der Maler der Frühromantik*, p. 11). I concur in his opinion on the first point, but I would hesitate on the basis of evidence that I shall introduce (p. 60) to exclude Runge's capacity for "romantic irony" as an agent for self-transcendence.

There is no question in my mind that the critical transitional area of the Ten-Point structure lies in Point Four. Whereas points One through Three might be called autistic or involuntary, hence automatic and not subject to disciplined learning or willful production, while points Five through Ten are the product of conscious organization, hence open to programmed learning, Point Four as the "terminus" of the previous points and the *terminus a quo* of the latter, forms the decisive threshold over which, suspended in delicate balance between the conscious and the unconscious, the crucial transformation from feeling to form takes place. Runge is quite aware of this and often voices his apprehension over the complexity of that point as when he says: "My major torture and pain, however, is how to go over from the conception and feeling to the form, without, in the process, losing both; i.e., instead of going over to the form, to cross over to the manner and thus, instead of remaining on the road, to fall into the moat, or, even if that moat should be dry, to lose all the beautiful prospects before the rampart" (letter to Daniel, Sept. 26, 1800, *H.S.*II, p. 57).

It is probably idle to add to this the obvious: anyone capable of piercing that rampart and beholding those prospects is an artist in the Rungian sense and need not trouble himself to read further in Runge's writings or in this essay, for that matter. Conversely, and for those who are not gifted in like manner, Runge holds out this consolation, which, incidentally, is typical of his thinking: "It is nothing and leads directly toward the decline of art to work from the outside in. Because who is to say that even if we are prevented by external circumstances from proceeding further with practice, we are also hindered from doing so in theorizing?" Note well "external circumstances!" In the absence of a contradictory statement in *Hinterlassene Schriften*, we can assume these to be either certain given pressing exigencies of daily life or limitations imposed by the magnitude of artistic talent and genius, or both.

This is a most important issue, for it puts to rest those critics who seek for the justification of Runge's theory only his own paintings and drawings. As has been stated in the Preface, this is patently not this writer's thesis. "The feeling," Runge continues, "aside from all works of art, can itself become a whole and thereby enable man to sustain the coherence within him; he will then, while viewing a perfect work of art, find the same coherence in it which he himself has known how to achieve, he will now be able calmly to enjoy it with pleasure, even if it should move him in the deepest; and this is the point of view, I believe, from which alone one must begin, without which no perfect composition is thinkable." And we might add: even if this "perfect composition" should never be achieved (letter to Böhndel, September 1801, *H.S.*II, p.82). A curious parallel to the "theoretical artist" is the "theoretical farmer." In a letter to his brother Gustaf (Hamburg, June 1808, *H.S.*I, p.208), who was an agronomist, Runge asks whether he might not just as well be a "farmer without land" as he himself is a "painter in a time when it is in bad taste to paint pictures."

Daniel writes (*H.S.*I, p.223) that on his deathbed the artist requested him to cut up and destroy his major painting *Der Morgen* (Grosse Fassung, 1809, oil on canvas, unfinished, reconstructed, 151 × 111.5 cm., Hamburg Kunsthalle, inv. No. 1022) because he thought that some things in it were wrong and could lead to the "spreading of errors." Daniel cut up the picture into nine parts but, of course, did not destroy them. The painting has only recently been reconstructed. Not nearly enough importance has been ascribed to this last wish of Runge, as it is mentioned only cursorily by biographers. Now, it seems that this incident proves again my contention that Runge distinguished between his theory and his practice. Whereas the former is an autonomous and universally valid construct (and was never recanted by Runge), the latter is considered inferior relative to the theory according to most critics, and also appeared that way to Runge himself. The chief reason for that is Runge's complex personal iconography which does not, in the final resolve, succeed in conveying the intended message. It is important, therefore, that we draw a line of demarcation between Runge's iconography and the present concern. That is, as a rule, never done by scholars.

If we ask ourselves what Runge seeks, art or the aesthetic experience, we could easily opt for the second, provided we understand Runge's concept of art as neither the artistic activity nor the ability to transform the raw and dead matter to the vehicle of the product of artistic fantasy, nor indeed as artistic activity itself, but rather as a constant striving toward the highest knowledge of art and the study of all things in their relation to human life. We would also have to understand Runge's approach to art as transcending aesthetics and see in it, rather, a system of ethics, a philosophy of human conduct and aspirations leading to the attainment of a moral ideal. Art to Runge is an instrument for the expression of the inexpressible. But he also knows the danger this attitude harbors for the production of works of art, which might forever be stillborn: "Anyone who reasons too early while producing a work of art, produces something cold and heartless; and any-one who contemplates about himself before it is time to do so fares the same way. We must really first love individual human beings from the bottoms of our hearts, before we can love humanity, otherwise it would be a love born of boredom" (letter to Daniel, May 15, 1802, *H.S.*II, p.132).

"Without love we cannot find either art or wisdom, only through love can we both speak to the soul of man and also understand art and any lan-guage of the soul, be it spoken in pictures, tones or words" (letter to his brother David, Nov. 21, 1801, *H.S.*II, p.97). Because we know that for Runge love is that viable force which is released into the world through religion, is art then for him tantamount to religion? He answers: "Religion is not art; religion is the highest gift of God, it can only be expressed more gloriously and more intelligibly through art."

We may compare this attitude to that of Friedrich Overbeck and his *Lukasbruderschaft* in Rome. Whereas Runge's confessed immanentism is the solid rock, the given constant, the primal moving power of all his ac-tions, including the source of his art which is intended to glorify God, *mutatis mutandis*, Overbeck and his followers considered art to be a holy temple service, an activity comparable to, even identical with religious wor-ship. It was a procedure designed to stimulate Christian piety rather than be the result of it. In that manner they put the cart before the horse. There is no basis for comparing Runge's and the Nazarenes' artistic motivations other than that which puts them at opposite poles on that issue: to the former, Christianity was the hypostasis of art, to the latter art was the entelechy of faith. Pauli says that, unlike the Nazarenes who were conver-tites and worked strictly in the framework of the church, Runge was a free agent, "the innocent child of the world to whom nature is holy because to him it is the obvious proof, even the mirror image of God" (*Philipp Otto Runges Zeichnungen*, p.23).

We have seen that the transition from the feeling to the form is of paramount importance. We might ask in a most general way—without becoming involved in a discussion of Runge's complex personal iconog-raphy and private world of symbolism at this point—what that "form" should resemble. Runge answers:

When I reproduce the world as it shows itself in my mind, who can tell me if I have reproduced it correctly? I have done it for myself, copied it from my real feeling, and that is how the thing stands; where I could not express it after the rule, I would rather have expressed it as I was able to, and where I was lacking something I would rather have said nothing or have said what I had to say badly, than well and according to the rule. Otherwise it would have been a lie and one is not supposed to lie (letter to Daniel, July 31, 1803, *H.S.*II, p. 232).

A comparison with Tieck urges itself upon us. Dürer (in *Franz Sternbalds Wanderungen*) speaks prophetically to Sternbald: "Don't you believe that it will be possible in future times to represent things and to express stories and feelings in a manner the likes of which we cannot even imagine now?" This is followed by an even more striking prediction, ominously suggestive of Expressionism and nonobjective abstract art, when Sternbald says to Bolz, after viewing the spectacle of a dazzling sunset: "Well, my friend, what could you say if an artist were to represent this wonderful scene in a painting? Here we see no action, no ideal, only glimmer and confused shapes which move about like almost unrecognizable shadows. But if you were to see the paintings, would you not be able to intuit the subject with powerful empathy?" And he continues a little later: "And that mood would then, just as it does now, fill out your whole inner being. There would be nothing left for you to desire, and yet, it would be nothing more than an artificial, almost trifling play of colors." And he closes his observations: "No, my friend, I am most profoundly convinced that art is like nature, it has more than one beauty" (in *Dichtung der Romantik*, pp.68, 218). Thus the task is set, the goal defined. Tieck may be the challenger in this. But Runge set out to reach it in his art and developed an art theory for it. A genuine revolution!

We can only see in Runge's sentiment the implication of a literal fiat for an Expressionistic, perhaps even abstract art which, being the visual equivalent of commonly held feelings and emotions, could become a direct "family language" comprehensible to all. ". . . Even if no one is particularly interested in your feeling, others must have it too within them, and if one person told it once to another it would seem even as clasping hands and looking into one another's eyes to show how things stir in our souls" (*H.S.*I, p.3). "Without the identical basis of feeling, no work of art, no music can be understood; anyone who continues to build on hearsay, builds upon a fundament which he does not know" (letter to Pauline, Dresden, 1801–04, *H.S.*II, p.179).

Runge of course refers to Neoclassical art when he speaks of "hearsay" and "unknown fundaments." That Runge did not err in his supposition that such a spontaneous family language in the visual arts is possible, or at least worthy of empirical experimentation, is demonstrated to us in three ways: first, in the eventual appearance of "action painting" or nonobjective abstract Expressionist art totally based on feeling in the twentieth century; second, in the startling over-all similarity and formal homogeneity of these productions; and third, in the demonstrated ease of impulsive "communication" and intuitive comprehension thereby achieved.

In the final resolve, however, the proper province for dealing with this whole problem area is not art history but experimental aesthetics and psychology. Only an effective technical terminology, a theoretical insight into the mechanics of psychic stimuli and responses, as well as exacting laboratory testing conditions could attempt to deal with the problem of Runge's hypothesis objectively and axiologically. Also the question whether nonobjective-abstract-expressionistic art really "expresses" the feeling of its creator, or whether it does not but rather relates to the spectator merely in the manner of an inkblot in the Rorschachian sense and stands, as finished work on the museum wall, in no emotional or intellectual content-bearing relationship to the artist, should best be studied in the laboratory.

While such a controlled verification of the functional efficacy of abstract and particularly nonobjective abstract art has, to my knowledge, so far eluded us, Runge's theory—in a language that reflects mid-twentieth-century tachistic sentiments—often intimates and occasionally forthrightly suggests the distinct possibility of just such a non-naturalistic approach to art. In the final resolve only a very careful analysis and interpretation of all the quoted material from Runge in this book, with the aim of plumbing the depth of Runge's implications, will provide the reader with all the arguments in support of my claim.

May I, however, at this point, indicate those aspects of Runge's theory which I believe are particularly telling in our present context. In the order of their appearance in the foregoing, these are: Runge's stress on the creative process and method over the finished work; the existential quality of his world ideology; the profundity of meaning with which he invests the relationships of abstract compositional elements; the spontaneity of attitude and execution which he counsels; his affirmation of childlike directness and naiveté; Point Seven of his "Ten-Point Program," his defense of sketchy and fragmentary art products; the primacy he attaches to the feelings of the artist and the surprisingly low priority which he gives to that which he actually produces; and the inviolable legitimacy with which he invests the private image in man's mind (cf. pp. 47, 49, 50, 53, 81, 82, 84, 88, 91, 96, 99).

And further, in the subsequent portions of this essay, other substantiating aspects are: according to Runge, the elements of art are within us, and he believes in the possibility of the psychological experiencing of the elements of form; he counsels on behalf of a total openness of symbolism free from all restrictions; to him art is a heightened product of nature;

color is in itself a movement and a natural force; his search for the dynamic, abstract, painterly, symbolic, and organic expression; his synesthetic experiencing of art and music; the implication of his color theory insofar as the free, associative, and symbolic meaning of colors and their nonobjective, psychological experiencing is concerned; his search for the fleeting and amorphous natural form that is by its very nature abstract and free; his assumption that all art must be based on the present moment in our existence with all its pains and pleasures (cf. pp. 111, 114, 117, 124, 128, Chap. V; pp. 160, 173, 178, 179, 207). May the above few examples suffice to establish a cogent analogy between Runge and contemporary aesthetics. These issues will be taken up repeatedly in the following discussion.

Runge scholarship has not, to my knowledge, interpreted Runge's "program" according to Surrealistic criteria in art. Yet we cannot deny that Runge's statements, taken as a whole, seem to lend themselves extremely well to such an interpretation. If Runge's theories point toward Expressionism and abstraction, it seems they do so in the direction of a hyper-real interpretation of the words. Not least of all, of course, do Runge's paintings, particularly his "Large Morning" (cf. Chapter V), impress us with their Surrealistic "flavor." They do so as a result of a startlingly uncommon constellation of common objects, the altered meaning of familiar objects by the strangeness of their location, the willful blending of reality with metaphor and symbol, and an over-all mood of enigma that would occur only in the domain of Morpheus. Yet, just as my previous attempt at linking Runge's oeuvre to primitivism, so also with Surrealism, my intention should be understood as a mere suggestion of the complexity of our problem rather than as a lucid "explanation." The great variety of interpretational and critical approaches that have been suggested by Runge scholarship attests in the final resolve to Runge's own creativeness. It will also become apparent in my discussion of Runge's iconography that the artist himself encouraged all to explore a great many avenues in "reading" his art.

Runge's very fine sense of romantic irony deserves special mention and comparison, above all, with Friedrich Schlegel, who saw irony as the true home of philosophy and as that form of the paradox which embodies greatness and beauty. Schlegel considered irony the constant change of self-creation and self-destruction, exactly, therefore, the process of nature (cf. "Fragmente" in *Athenaeum*, Stuttgart, 1960). Romantic irony became thus the agent by means of which the artist could transcend himself by willing the fate of his own imagination upon his creation and thus making himself stand to it in the same relationship as God stands to nature. (Compare Chapter III, for a different dimension of the same romantic attempt at self-deification.) How is it possible for a rational human being, even if he did consider himself to be a Romanticist, to desire the impossible, to obtain the Blue Flower of a Novalis, a Schlegel, a Runge, in short, to combine the real and the ideal? The answer is simple: it is irony as the last refuge and the highest insight into God's creation. This resignation to the inevitable, this flight from the emotional shock of the ultimate comprehension of the senselessness of existence, also found among the Romanticists its happy realization in religious worship. A letter to Daniel of April 14, 1802, rings with romantic irony in the finest sense of the word, that is, the capacity of the creator to transcend his creation and to will its fate fortuitously, even as nature unpredictably and by the whim of chance creates, alters, and destroys itself by "fate." Inasmuch as the letter is an important final comment on the March "Manifesto" it is advisable to reproduce it in its entirety.

I am sending you a fair copy of my long letter of March 9th. I have already received your answer to the first part of it. I can already imagine your opinion of the whole thing; you do not resent the things that may have gone partly or completely amiss. Let me compare the letter with a palette which is completed in all mixtures and ready for the job of painting. I rather sense already now that in this theory are mixed several hues which I cannot use at all and that others are missing completely; but as long as I cannot mix better ones I have to use what I have. Also, I do not understand at all why I should not erect rules and build whole theoretical systems; if I keep them to myself and am master over them, I can just as soon tear them down again. And if I remain with the metaphor of the palette: even the greatest master has, of the system which he has mixed for himself, also left over colors, which do not enter into the immortal work: therefore, it is merely a matter of my using the right things from the palette, the rest will be thrown out anyway. Fortunately I have copied this letter for myself because it was so long and because I also wanted to have its context together with your answer (*H.S.*II, p. 126).

III. THEORY

RUNGE'S testimony quoted so far may be taken as an indication that he seldom, if ever, speaks on one topic alone—only on religion or on art or on art history or on nature—but rather that he treats of all these matters and many more *simultaneously* and often in one and the same sentence. The following discussion will encounter even increased hindrances to logical ordering. It is impossible to order Runge's impulsive, tropological, synthesizing *Gestalt* approach to existence and art, his overflowing "stream of consciousness," into a scholarly disputation, lucidly organized into topics, without compromising the unique, truly romantic spirit of Runge, and thus, as it were, spilling the child with the bath. To compare Runge's unified world view once again to that of Böhme, we can say that the latter would no longer be mystical were his mysteries unraveled; it is also the paradox of Romanticism that increased analysis yields only increased confusion, because it is the nature of the paradoxical to be inconsistent with logic and common sense. Because, just as Böhme, Runge lacked the language discipline of a philosopher-scholar in the classic sense, and had to employ metaphor, parable, simile, and other such devices as stem, at least in part, from the primitivist's inability to reason coherently in abstract terms, his writings, just as those of the Silesian mystic, appear to the casual and even the intensive reader as the proverbial riddle, wrapped in enigma, shrouded in mystery.

Out of deference to their readers, Runge's biographers often check the seeming chaos of his feelings only to provide us with what appears to be Pandemonium of the mind. But whereas the legitimacy of that practice— the scholarly transference of the state of confusion from the province of the emotions to that of the mind—is at best questionable, that "seeming chaos" has a very strict inner logic. It is comparable to childlike phantasy, the architectural theorems of Gotham, to Laputan and Balnibarbian projections, make-believe nursery games and, for that matter, to romantic art itself: the little children enjoy the flower of German Romantic poetry, prose, and art best of all. They would if they could read the bigger words lose themselves equally well in Novalis's *Heinrich von Ofterdingen* as in Schlegel's *116th Fragment* or in the work of Runge, who even furnishes his paintings with little child figures perched on lilies, tulips, and chrysanthemums beckoning other children to join them there. As it stands, they do not lose out in the end: Grimms' fairy tales, some of which were written by Runge, provide the essence of all these productions, with wonders to spare.

Runge wrote, aside from several most delightful and humorous travel journals (cf. "Phantasien und Märchen," *H.S.*I, pp. 371 ff.), *Von dem Fischer un syner Fru*, containing satirical overtones to the megalomaniacal power hunger of Napoleon, and *Von dem Machandelboom*, a blood-curdling tale of good and evil locked in grizzly struggle destined by fate (cf. *H.S.*I, pp. 424 ff.; pp. 430 ff.). Both of these were adapted by the Grimm brothers and are considered by all to be the finest examples of the folktale genre existing in German literature. Some critics ascribe to Runge sympathies for Catholicism on the basis of his having introduced the pope in *Von dem Fischer un syner Fru* as that supreme temporal-spiritual power which cannot be usurped by any ambitious mortal for his private gains. I cannot take seriously an argument that proposes a qualitative judgment of a man's religious leanings on the basis of a folktale which he recorded on hearsay!

We do not want to disabuse the reader of the notion that a naïf, ingenuous, unsophisticated, even childlike approach to Runge appears to be the only one truly commensurate with his intentions. Yet, we must in steps of reasoned progression enter the realm of progressive unreason or that untoward province which Runge likened, in one jocular aside, to a "compact between himself and Satan crazily consummated in a moment of drunken abandon" (cf. letter to Daniel, July 10, 1803, *H.S.*II, p. 223).

As a natural corollary of his "Manifesto," we might cite anything else Runge has ever written on art, that corpus of writings being his "Theory," collectively speaking. Of considerable interest to us is Runge's "reading" of the history of art and his expectations, arising therefrom, of a new epoch in art, one based on landscape, and in the process at the turn of the eighteenth into the nineteenth century. As might be expected, Runge's fundamentalist understanding of I Genesis attributes to Lamech's three sons the initial invention and development of the arts (letters to Tieck, Dec. 1, 1802, *H.S.*I, pp. 25 ff.; to Daniel, Nov. 7, 1802, *H.S.*I, pp. 17 ff.; both make references to I Genesis 4, 20 ff.). Quotations from the Covenant at Mt. Sinai and the Ten Commandments, forbidding the fashioning of idols, are witnesses to Runge's deep-seated antipathy to traditional religious history painting with its anthropocentric imagery. Following his previously cited statement that "we are no longer Greeks," Runge says: "We see in the works of art of all times very clearly how the human race has changed, how the same time that was here once can never come back again." What Runge seems to say is in effect comparable to Heinrich Wölfflin's famous dictum concerning the reasons for stylistic change throughout history: "Not all is possible at all times." Runge counters neoclassicism by adding: "How can we conceive of such an unhappy idea as to want to recall the old art?" (*H.S.*I, p. 6). To Egyptian art Runge ascribes the "hardiness, iron-likeness and rawness" of the human race, to the Greeks the "feeling for religion and its dissolution into art" (ibid.).

"Michelangelo was the highest point in composition, the *Last Judgment* is the marking stone of the historical composition, Raphael already delivered much that was not purely historical in composition, the Madonna in Dresden [Sistine Madonna] is obviously only a feeling which he expressed by means of those well-known figures, after him nothing actually historical has been made, all beautiful compositions lean toward the landscape,—the Aurora by Guido" (ibid.).

"There has not been a single landscape artist who has expressed real meaning in his landscapes, who has brought allegories and clearly beautiful thoughts into a landscape. Who does not see the spirits upon the clouds at sunset? Who does not have the clearest thoughts in his soul?" (ibid.).

Dresdner elucidates as follows:

Runge pushes aside tradition insofar as it tries to push its way between the artist and the experience of nature. He endeavors to grasp nature exclusively through the organs of his personal feelings and individual life. He is not satisfied—as was the Rococo, an art still mightily effective during his time—to view and represent nature as the scene of acting man, i.e., in the manner of a spatial attribute of his being, but rather he seizes it first of all in her own autonomous existence, independent of man, and abandons himself to her; but then he takes possession of her through his own free mental power by letting her enter into his own inner life; thereby he interprets nature. And indeed this artistic principle which Runge expounds is a new and fruitful one. It is nothing else except the new, the modern feeling for nature which he imparts to his work (Dresdner, *Der Maler der Frühromantik*, p. 5).

Thus Runge expresses his belief that art moves historically away from historical representation and toward the expression of feeling, in short, progresses from objectivity toward subjectivity. G. W. F. Hegel's critical art history proposes in its essential arguments the same thesis, namely that art moves historically toward increased spirituality (cf. Hegel, "Vorlesungen über die Aesthetik," *Werke*). Frederick Coplestone says that Hegel's notion of romantic art in which "the spirit overflows, abandons the veils of the senses" is that of an art of Christendom and of the spirit; the typical romantic arts—painting, music, and poetry—will be adopted to express movement, action, and conflict (cf. Coplestone, *A History of Philosophy*, Vol. VIII, "Fichte to Nietzsche"). Moreover, it moves from classic anthropomorphism toward Romantic animism. Whereas classic art used the figure of man as an allegory of natural forces, the new Romantic Rungian art is to use nature as allegory of man. Runge expresses this historical change from classic homocentricity to Romantic animism thus:

At first people forced the elements and natural forces into the human figure, they always saw only in man the movement of nature; the proper historical province for them was to see in history itself only those mighty forces: that was history; the greatest picture which originated therefrom was the *Last Judgment*; all rocks became human figures, and the trees, flowers, and waters collapsed. Now the meaning falls more on the opposite. Just as even the philosophers are finding out how one imagines everything from one's own inner self, so also do we see or should see in each flower the living spirit which man imparts, and thereby landscape will come about, because all animals and flowers are only half there if man does not do his best with them; man forces thereby his own feelings upon the objects around him and thus all achieves meaning and language (*H.S.*I, p. 7).

The most eloquent witnesses to that unique imagination are A. Schopenhauer (cf. his "Die Welt als Wille und Vorstellung," *Sämtliche Werke*), and, of course, F. W. J. Schelling, whom Runge must have had in mind (cf. his "Identitätsphilosophie," *Schellings Werke*). Later Runge writes:

I feel very definitely that the elements of art can only be found in the elements as such and it is there that we must search. The elements as such, however, are within us. Thus all shall and must flow from our soul. We see the living spirit which man puts there, in every flower and that is how landscape is created. Because all animals and flowers exist only in part as long as man does not add his best to them. The pleasure which we have with the flowers still stems from paradise. Inwardly we always connect a meaning with the real flower. Once we see in all of nature only our own life, then it follows clearly, the right landscape can come about as completely opposed to the human or historical composition (letter to Daniel, Nov. 7, 1802, *H.S.*I, p. 16).

Runge links the history of religion closely to the history of art. It seems to him that the Greeks achieved the highest formal beauty at a time when their gods were perishing (Dresden, February 1802, *H.S.*I, pp. 7 ff.). Viewing all history in cyclical fashion, in which the climax and initial decline in religion triggers a sudden blossoming of the arts, Runge expands the theory to include the Renaissance which achieved the pinnacle of its perfection in art at a time when imminent spiritual dissolution threatened Catholicism. And Runge continues by adding: "In our time again something declines, we stand at the edge of all religions, the abstractions are falling down, all is more airy and light than anything seen so far, all urges toward landscape" (ibid.).

It is quite clear how these sentiments contradict the Nazarene program with its insistence on recreating the very art which Runge proposed to bury forever. F. Schlegel, perhaps the most persuasive advocate of the Nazarenes, suggests, in speaking about "hieroglyphics, true symbolic pictures," that "whoever has had the opportunity to have seen the allegorical drawings of the deceased Runge" will understand what "danger of going astray is implied in following his way which is based on nature hieroglyphics, torn loose from all historical and sacred tradition which, after all, forms the solid mother earth for the artist" ("Aufforderung an die Maler der jetzigen Zeit" in "Gemäldebeschreibungen aus Paris und den Niederlanden in den Jahren 1802–1804"; "Ansichten und Ideen von der Christlichen Kunst," *Sämtliche Werke*, Vol. 6). It is quite clear that Runge's views contradict the fully anthropocentric art of Cornelius and the School of Munich. Conversely, and with certain reservations in force, only Friedrich in seclusion and privacy seems to have perpetuated given aspects of the Rungian notions of an animistic-Romantic-Christian landscape art. Herbert von Einem suggests, "Runge's thoughts lead us directly to Caspar David Friedrich." And he continues: "In Friedrich's landscapes the new of which Runge speaks in anticipation has gained form and in them landscape painting reaches that significance toward which Runge had pointed that genre." (*Caspar David Friedrich*, p. 26. Compare Chapter V, page 102, for views which are contrary to those of Einem on this issue.)

The idea of the death of art which Runge expresses often suggests the necessity of either an organic disintegration or a willful, iconoclastic liquidation of art as the requisite first step in the direction of a new art. "Art must first again be scorned and considered to be completely worthless before anything can be derived from it again" (letter to Daniel, June 19, 1803, *H.S.*I, p. 46).

Was not that art which is perfect merely the messenger of something to come which is better? You say that you cannot understand that it would be a great future for art, if all works of art were now to perish. It would not be good for art, but for us. I know well how beautiful art is and how wonderfully it occupies man. And yet, I do not want to be an artist in this respect. I know what I give, but I also know what I receive. If it were necessary to destroy the works of art now, they would be destroyed. Now they still stand for a while but their time will come and mine too. But how can art grow but that it becomes necessary for the human race to use it? What is said is perfect, what is said for the second time is fine in libraries or in granaries. In both no seed will thrive to new plants. The granary decays and collapses. Much grain might grow after the fall. First thrive for the Kingdom of God and for His justice and all else will come your way. The practical and mechanical must also find their bases in our feeling. Once we receive in our soul the foreboding of our connection with the universe, through our holy enthusiasm for God and once the living child is born in this bliss through our personal strength, so also at the same moment occurs the construction of the figures. And our manipulations will manage to hold up the clothes which God will give us too (letter to Quistorp, Aug. 30, 1803, *H.S.*I, p. 237).

A most important letter in this context is one which Runge wrote to his brother Gustaf in December 1807 (*H.S.*I, pp. 77 ff.). Runge elaborates at considerable length a great many interconnected matters, the leading ideas being the following. So that an artist may convey to another person a "total effect" of the spiritual impression a given natural scene has made upon him in a manner that does not constitute a "successive narration," he is obliged to use "characteristic signs" (or symbols) which he puts in such particular constellations relative to each other as are compatible with his feelings. (Compare Goethe's "Laokoon," *Schriften zur Kunst*; and Lessing's *Laokoon oder über die Grenzen der Malerei und Poesie, Werke*, as influences on Runge's argumentation despite his ostensible opposition to these men.) Runge conceives of art as a "heightened product of nature": "Thus only that person who regards the most beautiful works of art of the past as heightened products of nature, can really originate art anew. Because just as the formation in art can thus be made more extensive and engage deeper into the essence of all knowledge, and just as the spirit is thus liberated from the conventional bonds of opinion, so also will the practice of art be liberated to move evermore daringly" (1806 [?], *H.S.*I, p. 72). He regards the elements of art as the "elements as such" (above, p. 65).

From the just stated reasons and because such unisonal Romantic generalizations can only be mystically intuited but never learned, it follows that these "characteristic signs" or symbols (as in Point Four of the "Manifesto") must also come to the artist semi-autistically or not at all. Runge continues to write that these "characteristic signs" require in their specific character "analogy" to the "total effect" which they are intended to convey because "otherwise they would not be characteristic." In literature, Runge claims, this is achieved through the dramatic juxtaposition of persons and their characteristics and through the dramatic unfolding of the action. In art this is done through a constellation of form, positioning, and expression of the figures in relation to each other in such a manner that thereby and through the "characteristic parts of the whole" is produced the "total effect."

Runge follows this up by an exposition of the "physiognomic expressions" of the figures and, much more important, by a discussion of color and man's ability to experience color unconsciously in a symbolical manner. As for physiognomics, there is good reason to believe that Runge (just as Goethe) was drawn into the spell of J. C. Lavater, the father of physiognomics. His statements seem to corroborate that he had seen Lavater's, at the time most popular, *Physiognomische Fragmente zur Beförderung der Menschenkenntnis und Menschenliebe*. As for Runge's color theory, this discovery is generally considered his important original contribution to the "psychological" study of color. (Compare P. F. Schmidt, *Philipp Otto Runge, Sein Leben und sein Werk*, pp. 92 ff.)

According to Runge, the old "plastic artists," as he calls them, relied entirely on "form" and "expression" to suggest "great ideas" which they perceived by their "intimate penetration into the secrets of nature," but did not use "signs" or symbols. Therefore, it appears to him that one must not compare the perfection of classic sculpture with that of the "newer art." He intimates briefly also an interesting speculation concerning the historic succession of artistic media or the question whether sculpture or painting "came first," while choosing the first. Riegl agrees with him (cf. *Stilfragen, Grundlegungen zu einer Geschichte der Ornamentik*). Runge suggests that the ancient sculptors considered the "basic forces" of natural phenomena as analogies of their own passions and desires and therefore relied entirely upon "human imagery" in the expression of the invisible forces operative in nature. And because the ancients also conceived of their gods in the same anthropocentric fashion, the ancient man-centered art represented a total harmonious balance and fusion of "thought, medium and subject." But as soon as painting was introduced, that inherently harmonious circle was destroyed. In this context Runge presumably speaks of painting only as decoration for sculpture (e.g., polychrome pediments, etc.). This view leaves out the painting of the primitives (of which Runge could have had no knowledge), of the Egyptians, Greeks, Romans, and others, which was not used in that "superficial" decorative manner but as an independent medium.

The complete ruin of the "old art" did not occur before the perfection of the "purest representation through line"; that happened, according to Runge, either already in ancient Greece which perfected the expression through line beyond anything else, or, more recently, with Raphael. Thus at a time when line had reached the highest perfection, "man's heart opened in the center of color," so that he could no longer find the solution to his artistic problems in the "line" of the ancients but had to forge ahead and unlock the secrets of color and light.

Because, Runge believes, we have had such small regard for "all new discoveries in color" and because we lacked the courage "to leave the old and to find the ancient eternal basis of art in the new"—which is not really new but actually "more ancient than the ancient" itself—we are at present (i.e., the late eighteenth and early nineteenth centuries) caught up in a hopeless situation, a cul-de-sac, as it were (letter to Gustaf, Dec. 22, 1807,

WE THREE

1805, destroyed by fire, oil on canvas
100×122 cm.
H. K. Inv. No. 1014

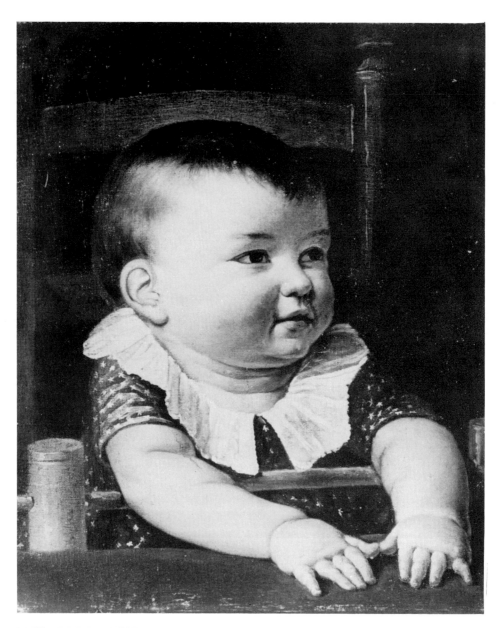

THE ARTIST'S SON, OTTO SIGISMUND

1805, oil on canvas
40×33.6 cm.
H. K. Inv. No. 1003

STARNO AND SWARAN BEFORE LODAS' STONES OF MIGHT

1805, pencil and pen and ink
52.7 × 75 cm.
H. K. Inv. No. 34143

REST ON THE FLIGHT INTO EGYPT

1805/1806, oil on canvas, unfinished
98 × 132 cm.
H. K. Inv. No. 1004

THE HÜLSENBECK CHILDREN

1805/1806, oil on canvas
130.5× 140.5 cm.
H. K. Inv. No. 1012

THE HÜLSENBECK CHILDREN (Detail)

THE HÜLSENBECK CHILDREN (Detail)

THE ARTIST'S PARENTS

1806, oil on canvas
194 × 131 cm.
H. K. Inv. No. 1001

THE ARTIST'S PARENTS (Detail)

THE ARTIST'S PARENTS (Detail)

ST. JOHN THE APOSTLE (Study for ST. PETER ON THE SEA)

black and white crayon on yellowish paper
39.2×28 cm.
H. K. Inv. No. 34161

ST. PETER ON THE SEA

1806/1807, oil on canvas, unfinished
116×157 cm.
H. K. Inv. No. 1007

MORNING (Small Version)

1808, oil on canvas
106×81 cm.
H. K. Inv. No. 1016

AURORA (Study for MORNING, small version)

1807, pencil and pen and ink
62.7× 44.7 cm.
H. K. Inv. No. 23701

AMARYLLIS

1808, oil on canvas on cardboard
56×30.2 cm.
H. K. Inv. No. 2032

THE JOYS OF HUNTING

1808/1809, pen and ink and watercolors
95.3×62.8 cm.
H. K. Inv. No. 1019

*H.S.*I, p. 80). Runge thus naturally saw in neoclassicism a dead end beyond which nothing new could be developed, and in color, which neoclassicism neglects, the beginning of the new road. Runge thinks that color is not "matter as a stone or a piece of wood" but that it is, rather, an entity which "in itself is movement and a natural force which relates to the form as tone relates to the word."

Runge voices a felt need for a systematic approach: "One can easily see that nothing would be more desirable than to have discovered an order by means of which all natural phenomena which we perceive by the sense of sight could be explained, an order which would also list the means which we possess in order to represent something in such a manner that the analogy of these means with the forces of nature would become apparent." We shall see in due course that Runge meant what he said and that he embarked on a lifelong and successful systematic theory of color for use by artists. Runge concludes this long letter by saying that while such colorists or, shall we say, "painterly artists" as Correggio and members of the Dutch School understood color intuitively, yet they did not systematically posit in writing their theories for the benefit of posterity because they may not have understood color too clearly and thus were unable to effect a "completely harmonious" resolution of the problem. At any rate, whatever they did know is now lost and that "only important science for painting must now be rediscovered or discovered anew."

It is our plan to develop successively the major spheres of interest according to the importance Runge attaches to them. In this regard, we found religious faith as preceding all other concerns and giving birth to a romantic-mystical awareness of man in relation to the universe. Second, we saw in the "Manifesto" Runge's attempt to explain art as flowing semi-automatically out of that faith and this presentiment, in short, out of that metaphysical infrastructure, collectively speaking. Third, we found emanating from Runge's "reading" of the history of art and religion arguments in favor of a new approach to art based on a thorough understanding of color fortified by a new non-anthropomorphic or romantic-animistic symbolism. The last two concerns will lead us directly to the specific discussions of Runge's color theory and his mythographic landscape art and personal iconography. Both matters will be taken up separately in Chapters IV and V.

But first, let us take up a number of related questions including, above all, Runge's general views on nature and landscape. Inasmuch as Runge, as has been seen, equates a work of art and natural phenomena as arising out of the same divine stimulus, he also speaks of both in the same manner; that is, neither should be imitated but rather intuited, or more specifically, we must intuit the Old Masters' intuition. May a few telling quotations suffice:

I say, when we learn to recognize in the nature of our own drives the deep feeling which motivated those great artists inwardly and which produced in them their method, as well as recognize [in our drives] the great phenomena of nature, there is no doubt but that the idea of the whole practice [of art] will appear to us as a viable means that must correspond to all our perceptions [or sensations] (1808 [?], *H.S.*I, p. 73; also cf. Chapter II and letter dated 1807 or 1808, *H.S.*I, p. 104). . . . . In that manner a painting can stand in nature as a second creation the perfection of which will appear all the greater, the deeper the painter penetrates into the elements of natural phenomena (in "Die Elemente der Farben," *H.S.*I, p. 84). . . . Art stands as a second nature (ibid., *H.S.*I, p. 85).

However, Schrade casts uncertainty on the basic Rungian proposition when he doubts that the subject of landscape can be made compatible with the specifically Christian notions about life in the first place: "The romantic elevation of landscape to the most significant object of Christian art indeed represents one of the strangest perversions of the values of subject matter from the point of view of that which until then had been valid and obligatory" (*Die romantische Idee von der Landschaft als höchstem Gegenstande Christlicher Kunst*, p. 1). Why? Because, of course, according to the Christian idea of life nature is merely temporal, perishable, even evil and should be overcome and conquered by the Christian Warrior. It is, however, precisely in his attitude toward nature (note well: not landscape) that Runge betrays the modern Christian standpoint as opposed to the traditional one of which Schrade speaks.

Out of Runge's notion of the identical nature of the "basic material elements" in the makeup of both nature and art, a strange situation develops whereby it is at times difficult, at times even impossible, to tell at any given moment whether Runge speaks about art or about nature. He writes at one point: "If I am supposed to show you now what I am trying to say, you must, as difficult as this may seem to you, move away from art and toward nature, and the drive to produce something beautiful in art must first compel your ability to find the pure pleasure in the formation of the phenomena itself which, in turn, will also unlock for you your own inner creativity" (*H.S.*I, p. 73).

This notion expressed by Runge leads us to speculate about two distinct problems. One is the necessity for the rational, analytic penetration of the makeup of nature; hence, science as a basic prerequisite for art (Runge's scientific investigations are largely deposited in those parts of his color theory where he does not dwell on metaphysics, mystical color symbolism, etc.). It should be added here that Runge was influenced in his "natural science" by his friend Heinrich Steffens, the Norwegian-German physicist-chemist whose many publications, particularly those in his special field of geognosy, were widely known. In 1807 Steffens lived in Hamburg.

In Steffen's geognosy, strains of exact science converge with those of a metaphysical vitalism resulting in the romantic hybrid discipline known as *Naturphilosophie* ("nature philosophy") in which Schelling, the friend of both Steffens and Runge, achieved lasting fame. Repeatedly we find expressed in *Hinterlassene Schriften* views and concepts which reflect the entelechy of the two philosopher-scientists in the mirror of the artist's own and Böhmian mysticism. (For the Steffens-Runge cooperation in the investigation of color see Chapter IV.)

The other problem is a most interesting prototypal *Gestalt* theory concerning the basic psychology relating to the process of optical vision and rational conception. It is surprising that this concern has not been detected, to my knowledge, by Runge's biographers. What Runge implies is that we do not perceive in a series of individual sense impressions which form a mosaic of pictures in our mind, but rather that we perceive in integrated patterns which cannot be analyzed from a knowledge of their parts only, and that these patterns transcend in importance and meaning the sum total of their parts (cf. *H.S.*I, pp. 148 ff.).

In a section of *Hinterlassene Schriften* entitled "Rubrics" (*H.S.*I, pp. 190 ff.), Runge successively develops the matters just discussed, in several succinct paragraphs that seem to express his essential contention. Here is an abstract of what he writes: (1) A man is not born so as to be able to arrive at art without much effort, just as he does not see, but first must learn how to see. (2) However, the consciousness of seeing robs him of freedom, for as he now knows what he sees, he also knows what he does not see. (3) Apprenticeship, eclecticism, and scientific probings kill off completely the last traces of an indigenous art. (4) The understanding of the old masters must spring from an understanding of man and natural phenomena. (5) Science must spring from the desire to understand nature because upon that science is built the living creation. Runge concludes by saying (6) that art practice cultivates the perception of art and nature; (7) that perceiving art and nature causes the desire also to practice art, and (8) that therefore the good art school should encourage both practice and perception depending on the native aptitude of the student (*H.S.*I, p. 189). A paragraph preceding the "Rubrics" expresses most concisely what Runge means: "As the unaffected sense derives pleasure from a well-put and vital expression, even though it may be somewhat one-sided, nevertheless, our reason urges us toward completeness . . . because only then will we have a good instrument with which to receive a deeper and purer glance into the grandeur of existence" (*H.S.*I, pp. 189 ff.). Runge was keenly interested in technique. He often writes at length about the intricacies of the production of pigments, techniques of glazing, *velare*, stippling, scumbling, and others (cf. letter to Böhndel, Jan. 13, 1805, *H.S.*I, pp. 58 ff.). More significantly, Runge's concept of the art school points directly to the twentieth-century Bauhaus pedagogy in encouraging a departure from specialization, departmentalization, and fractionization of the artistic disciplines, and from the division existing between art and life as a whole, while counseling for a "totally unified," coherent approach.

The brilliant essay by Gunnar Berefelt (*Bemerkungen zu Ph.O. Runge's Gestaltungstheorie*) deserves extensive mention in our present context to illuminate Runge's "theory of design" from the incisive vantage point of one of Runge's most gifted critics. Berefelt says that Runge's *Gestaltungstheorie* ("formative theory") sees art as an instrument which can be played effectively so as to duplicate the artist's feelings in the spectator. The composing must be codified in such a way as to allow for no ambiguities or "missing of the intended message." Runge regarded nature as the manifest revelation of a religious-cosmogonic higher reality and art as the human transformation of that function of nature which realizes or manifests ideas as such. In that context we can apply to Runge the "creative imitation" concept developed by Alexander Baumgarten (1714–1762, author of *Aesthetica*, 1750), considered the father of modern aesthetics, which establishes a "working analogy" between art and nature. (Compare my discussion of the same problem in relation to Schelling's and Goethe's theories, Chapter II.) Thus the artist must organize his picture with artistic elements which are analogous in their effects to those achieved by nature, or, more precisely, with those elements which constitute the immanent reality of nature. A work of art, therefore, according to Runge, should be composed of those elements which have given nature her symbolic and God-revealing power.

Berefelt further distinguishes between Runge's use of individual, object-related symbols (*Objectsymbole*)—and their combination in complex allegories—and his later attempts at condensing the meaning of a picture into a unified and single symbolic statement to be experienced at a glance and not in successive reading stages. Traditional art was allegorical, anthropomorphic, and plastic. The new art must be symbolic, organic, and painterly. Runge seeks the dynamic-abstract-symbolic rather than the mimetic-realistic-reproductive landscape. The artist, in order to find analogies between form and content must seek creative means, that is, means of design, composition, and color, which correspond and are contiguous with those "idea manifestations" which are immanent in nature. But Runge never really arrived at that point in his practice because he only remained with the first stages leading to such an art, namely, the resolution of problems relating to optical reproduction. So far my annotated synopsis of Berefelt's summation.

This obsession with completeness, this expansive, all-inclusiveness, this psychologically seemingly excessive desire to "perceive the grandeur of existence" at a glance, this sweeping gesture which reaches out to embrace all the knowledge of all times at a single moment in life while brushing aside the concrete as well as doubts about the concrete—these are characteristics which confront us in every page that Runge has written. They are an involuntary, quasi-megalomaniacal trait born from a long history of German mysticism, reaching its emotional-poetic crescendo during the period of Early German Romanticism. As such they are common to all the best representatives of that movement. That mystic-poetic ingredient, coupled with natural philosophy, "nature science," and neo-Platonic idealism in the framework of a highly disciplined logical-semantical apparatus, became the substructure from which rose the soaring mental edifices of the transcendentalist philosophers to heights that still stagger the imagination. Runge built that edifice for the corpus of the visual arts, but, unfortunately for the present-day reader, owing to his scholastic limitations, he did not furnish it with the requisite skeletal infrastructure to make it readily intelligible to all people at all times.

Runge's concepts taken as a whole are not merely a theory but a work of art, because they have a beautiful inner logic and interdependence of thoughts, are therefore purposive within, although they may not necessarily be demonstrably purposive without, as ultimately indeed his whole system, or non-system as he would rather have christened it, may be patently purposeless. Must we not also ask ourselves the ultimate question as to the real purpose of art, particularly of art today, an art cast adrift and absolved from its agelong servitude to the Church? To think that the humble Immanuel Kant could have triggered such an overwhelming response among the men of the period by demonstrating man's inability to know the "thing in itself"! Are we to see in Romantic idealism an emotional overcompensation for that demonstrated human shortcoming? A matter of pride, then? Are we to see in the Romantic thought structures a temporary nervous breakdown of Germany's intelligentsia? That may be as it will. It is sufficient to say that our present age is hostile to metaphysical speculation. The pitilessly severe philosophy of the twentieth-century—with the exception of Existentialism which does not claim to be a self-consistent systematized philosophy and which Runge and his friend Schelling helped to formulate in its incipient form—separates with the razor-sharp surgical knives of psychologists, logicians, linguists, mathematicians, and other "specialists," body from soul; that latter flees ever deeper toward its mysterious origin. Those among us who are dissatisfied with the state of affairs of this fractionized, ice-cold, mechanistic, and humanly uninspiring methodology may find refuge in philosophy as world ideology as expounded by the German Romanticists of the early nineteenth century.

In the context of the Romanticists' desire to engulf the whole broad spectrum of human sensations into a unified and intensified experience, synesthesia ranks paramount. It has been a predominant stylistic device used by a great many Romantic poets and prose writers and has been a critical concern of most literary historians. In Runge the trait of synesthesia is so pronounced as to urge upon some writers the need to view it in the light of abnormal psychology (e.g., Aubert, *Runge und die Romantik*, p.62; cf. Schmidt, *Philipp Otto Runge, Sein Leben und Sein Werk*, p.77). We shall come to speak of this phenomenon once again when we discuss Runge's *Tageszeiten* and iconography. At this point a few general observations may suffice. Runge devotes a separate theory to the analogy of colors and tones, which may be found as an appendix to his color theory ("Gespräche über die Analogie der Farben und Töne," *H.S.*I, pp. 168 ff.). In it the musical octave is compared to the value range of colors as literally analogous. The same interest, incidentally, is expressed by Goethe in his *Farbenlehre*, although he limits the possibilities of the analogy more within the bounds imposed by the logic of concrete facts and data. Reflecting upon Haydn's *Seasons*, after one of the concerts he attended frequently, Runge says: "For the maintenance of one's pure nature and simultaneously for the innocence of one's mind" it is necessary to recognize "the symbolism of the proper poetry, i.e., the inner music of the three arts, in word, line and color." He continues: "Music, after all, is that which we call harmony in all the arts. Thus there must be music through words in a beautiful poem, just as there must be music in a beautiful picture and in a beautiful building or any kind of idea which is expressed through lines" (letter to Daniel, April 6, 1803, *H.S.*I, p. 42). We cannot but liken this idea of Runge to Kandinsky's doctrine of the musical basis of the visual arts expressed in his *Über das Geistige in der Kunst* of 1912.

Following the recital of a duet, Runge makes a most curious remark: "I have just heard the pair singing; she held the full tone so long, and Benelli sang in-between; that means to paint on a gold ground" (letter to Daniel, Dec. 21, 1802, *H.S.*II, p. 188). He expands shortly thereafter this hyperbolic metaphor thus: "I feel how everything in my innermost depth comes to life; thus also the earth lives within and the happy tones hop out from the depth of flowers: thus [emanates] the joyous life from the fingers of an artist" (ibid.).

Runge had made friends in Dresden with a young composer named Berger and he received from him "instructions in music," for Runge considered it to be of great advantage "for an artist also to be at home in the other arts" (letter to his father, March 26, 1802, *H.S.*II, p.122). On one occasion Runge takes the opportunity to describe at length the ceremony in which all the senses through words, pictures, sculptures, music, "choreography," and exotic scents in the framework of monumental architecture are treated simultaneously (letter to his father, Dec.7, 1801, *H.S.*II, p. 101). Runge often visited the Catholic churches in Dresden and was very much impressed by the mass as an aesthetic experience (letters to Daniel, Aug. 7, 1801, *H.S.*I, p. 79; Sept. 12, 1801, *H.S.*I, p. 85). All writers on Runge agree that the experience of the Catholic mass contributed in large part to Runge's ideational formation of the total work of art, because in the church he saw the practical feasibility of such a project.

On the occasion of thinking about his *Tageszeiten*, he makes this startling comment: "As to my four pictures, the general idea of it and what can develop out of it: in short, once it becomes expanded, it will be an abstract painterly fantastic-musical poem with choirs, a composition for all three arts collectively, for which architecture should raise a completely special building" (letter to Daniel, Feb. 22, 1803, *H.S.*II, p. 202). As to the style of architecture he would use, he suggests that it would be a "continuation of the Gothic rather than the Greek" (letter to Daniel, June 3, 1803, *H.S.*II, p. 220). His profound impression of the Cathedral of Meissen (letter to his mother, June 15, 1803, *H.S.*II, p. 221) may very well have been the decisive stimulus for this architectural stylistic predilection.

Runge's insistence on the "Gestalttheoretical" scientific study and intuitive awareness of the maximum possible revelations of natural phenomena (as witness his color theory)—the resultant collective recept transcending in importance and meaning the sum total of all the parts making up ontic beings in nature—is as much an indigenous concomitant of his synthesthesia, as his *Gesamtkunstwerk* ("total work of art") theory is a natural result of both. No other vehicle of artistic expression really could serve the supra-inclusive, omnifarious demands he made of art. Synesthesia, the simultaneity and correspondence of sensory stimuli evoked by specific sensations, developed as it was in Runge to the point of sheer oversensibility, caused him to pair sound and sight and, as mutually complementary, the arts dealing with these properties: that psychological tendency and the impressions of the pageantry and "sensory feast" of the mass produced in the crucible of his tireless romantic fantasy the idea of the total work of art in the framework of a special architectural environment more than fifty years before Wagner and some hundred and twenty years before the Bauhaus.

It is, of course, of the greatest interest for us to know how Runge proposed to instrument such a highly ambitious project into reality. To pursue this question, we must turn to Runge's ideas regarding schools of art and the training of artists. We have already seen that he considered it vitally important that the academy, from which he himself had turned in disgust, teach both perception, i.e., knowledge and insight, as well as practice. (In this regard compare also his letter to Daniel, Feb. 17, 1801, *H.S.*II p. 66.) It is well known that European academies in the pursuit of studio action, if not necessarily in their more ethereal speculations, ever since the days of LeBrun concentrated on practice to the nearly exclusive detriment of perception. In addition, Runge had long desired to create a professional artists' cooperative or *Werkstatt* on the order of the Italian

75

Renaissance *bottega*, based on the realities and practical exigencies of civic existence. "If I could only," he writes, "in some way realize my dreams to instruct about ten different young people in their study" (letter to Klinkowström, Jan. 24, 1810, *H.S.*I, pp. 179 ff.).

It was Runge's wish to re-create for his time the institution of the old workshop as conducted by Raphael and his school, for example (ibid.; cf. letter to Daniel, Dec. 28, 1802, *H.S.*II, pp. 189 ff., in which Runge discusses his plans for a new art school). Individual members of the school, architects, sculptors, and painters, each according to his particular talents, would be encouraged to develop their natural proclivities to the fullest; thereafter each would contribute his share in the creation of decorative projects and the realization of monumental, total works of art. It is interesting in this context to note that Runge does indeed allow for the fusion of monumental and decorative art and, in theory, makes way for the fusion of these divergent artistic enterprises. He often refers to his *Tageszeiten* simultaneously as "room decorations" and monumental productions, thereby also simultaneously raising the stature of the former while assuring the public acceptance of the latter as practical propositions in the service of environmental beautification.

Isermeyer compares the actualization of the artists' cooperative under Friedrich Overbeck in such of their fresco cycles as, for example, the Casa Bartholdy and Casino Massimo projects in Rome, with Runge's unrealized plan of a "school." The former, he says, sought cooperation of equals, the latter subordination of minor talents under Runge's supreme guidance and planning (C. A. Isermeyer, *Philipp Otto Runge*). It is, of course, equally well known that the over-all artistic cohesion and compositional unity of the Rome projects suffered enormously for precisely the reasons Isermeyer states. The question we have to ask here is whether it is at all possible to have a "democratically" oriented artists' cooperative where all participate equally, shall we say, by committee decision or ballot casting, on decisions effecting the configurations of works of art such as monumental decorative projects, or whether such attempts are not doomed to failure right from the start.

In the instance of the Nazarene projects, the individual participating artists worked independently and freely and competed with each other within the framework of a thematic structure determined by an a priori decision by all. The over-all results, in their piecemeal and disjointed effect, are commensurate with this independence of initiative of the individual participants. Can we imagine the workshop production of a Raphael, a Rubens, a David guided by a "steering committee" and executed by dozens of freewheeling entrepreneurs? Runge must have intuited the illogic and impracticability of such an organization.

Walter Gropius said: "Architects, sculptors, painters, we all must return to handicraft! Because there is no art without vocation" (quoted from H. M. Wingler, *Das Bauhaus,* and the herein reproduced "Manifest und Programm des Staatlichen Bauhauses in Weimar," April 1919). We can readily see from this how advanced Runge's thinking was. He was aware of the fact that the fragmentation of artistic disciplines occurred in relatively recent times. He refers constantly to the School of Raphael which viewed the two as natural concomitants in art. Runge stands on solid historical ground, as in addition to the School of Raphael, the School of Dürer, of Fontainebleau, of Versailles, to name only the most famous, can be cited as precedents for his plan. But the nineteenth century saw the schism widen. Such men as Schinkel, Semper, Cole, Ruskin, Morris, van de Velde, Horta, and Behrens followed Runge in attempts at bridging the gap between art and craft. But only Gropius and the Bauhaus accomplished the task in reality.

The popularizing of his concept of art as combining the impulse for pleasure with noble aesthetic aspirations, was especially dear to Runge's heart. In this regard, Runge can be seen as forming the link between eighteenth-century pleasure-oriented aesthetics with nonhedonistic, ethics-oriented, and broadly psychologically responsive modern aesthetics. The task of removing his art from the narrow confines of the private circle of devotees gathered around him, and making it available to the public at large, loomed urgently in his mind (e.g., *H.S.*II, p. 190; *H.S.*I, pp. 26, 67). Therefore, M. J. Friedländer seems to be mistaken in the case of Runge when he says: "Eccentric, unsociable, with a modesty of manner behind which there not infrequently lurked a spiritual arrogance—such were many of the German painters, Wasmann, Runge, Fohr, Rohden, Olivier. . ." (Friedländer, *Landscape, Portrait, Still-Life*). I must confess surprise and amazement at this famous art historian's opinion of Runge. Besides, Runge unsociable? Gregarious would be more correct. Modest? Not really; on the contrary: on the basis of testimony by those who knew him he was exceptionally straightforward and sure of himself.

Runge knew that he stood at the beginning of a new road. But he also realized that he would not be able to see the ultimate goal of the new art which he was ushering in. His, he thought, was essentially the task of educator and guide.

What I know about art as a matter of certainty is of such nature, that, were I to tell people about it, they would surely declare me crazy and silly. But because I surely know that it is the truth, it is best that I do not say that which I myself can only grasp at times of an intensified mood, but rather that I prepare the public first via the road which I myself have taken and in that manner it will one day be possible to express the whole thing. Well, one thing is certain, my two hands are many too few to execute all that which I can do, and it is even more certain that many talented people roam the world who are not doing anything or who have nothing to do. I am thinking about having those hands join me in the following manner: the whole taste and fancy of today is devoted to elegance, decoration, and ornamentation; now, if I were to pack into this airy stuff the most solid of things?; and that would come easy to me as I already have successfully designed beautiful room decorations [i.e., murals] which, after all, express my whole idea of art . . ." (letter to his father, Jan. 13, 1803, *H.S.*I, p. 29).

At another point, Runge assures us that he would see to it that his decorative projects would appeal to people so much as to make patrons out of many of them. First, Runge planned the incorporation of this scheme of decorative projects into the workshop idea as such. Second, he envisioned the harmonious resolution of such single projects by a community of artists through cooperative effort under his over-all guidance. Finally, he promised to supply a continuously flowing stream of ideas emanating from his own fantasy. Such is the artist's ambitious scheme, his enthusiastic projection for a fuller and richer concept of art based on the fusion of fine and applied arts in the service of ethical and practical goals (ibid., p. 30). Unfortunately, Runge's short life, his illness, and the economic hardships of the times prevented his plans from reaching fruition and his intention to form an art school with W. Tischbein and Hardorff from going beyond the planning stage. With the exception of his Copenhagen and Dresden periods which he spent as a student, Runge lived in the "provinces" artistically and culturally speaking. Had he had the opportunity during the period of the attainment and crystallization of his independent plans to have lived, instead of in isolation, in such a city as Dresden, Vienna, or Rome, he would also have had a good chance to rally followers to his cause and to have made his influence felt. Pauli, for one, seems to think so also (cf. Pauli, *Philipp Otto Runges Zeichnungen*, p. 25). We can only guess at what might have been had Runge's passionate commitment to hard work not been checked by extraneous circumstances.

Runge also often reflects on the union of the multifarious artistic "sciences." "I am thinking more and more how I could bring about the union of the various artists, and that can only happen if they aid each other in their scientific knowledge, whereby scientific knowledge could really blossom; this serious thoroughness is the only road by which our times can accomplish anything" (letter to Goethe, Sept. 23, 1809, *H.S.*I, p. 178). In a letter to Schelling in Munich, Runge further elaborates on the necessity of combining science and art: "I see only too clearly how the little bit of art we have, which we can carry on now, stands on weak legs, and that the most necessary thing in our time certainly is the connection between the scientific results in the practice of art with the general scientific ideas and to raise them to their level" (Feb. 1, 1810, *H.S.*I, p. 158). One of the fundamental concepts of Bauhaus pedagogy was to bring art into the mainstream of contemporary science and technology. It is amazing how Runge pre-empted seemingly the whole Bauhaus program.

In the subsequent paragraphs of his letter to Schelling, Runge bewails the practice of specialization and "secret mongering" in the classic academies where the totality of art is not only not recognized but conscientiously prevented by the professors from ever materializing into actuality. Thus, the individual artistic disciplines are reduced to handiwork and to "lousy bags of tricks," drained of their viability and debased to the level of mere manual skills. And Runge continues with a statement that rings with the fervor of a Walter Gropius: "It could easily be demonstrated how a master with several friends and students could bring to light beautiful things if they united in their studies as architects, sculptors, and painters."

Runge had a keen understanding of the essential elements of the various artistic disciplines, and he went well beyond the mere statement that artists of all persuasions and media should unite. *Hinterlassene Schriften* are punctuated by insistent references to parallelisms of method and purpose of the various arts. It is of interest to us how Runge understood the connection between the arts, because it is of universal pedagogical application. At one point Runge gives us this summary: it is his first scientific task to universalize in theory the most common and primary natural effects regarding optics for the purpose of using such means toward practical artistic ends. By applying the identical basic idea to architecture, sculpture, and painting we shall learn to distinguish these three kinds of expression. And Runge continues:

The difference between these three arts will be nothing new to anyone who has looked at anything at all by virtue of the fact that this distinction is based upon the exigencies of the basic characteristics of sight, namely upon the ability to distinguish proportions or figures (architecture, rhythm), movement or form (sculpture, melody), medium (painting, tone) which are all as one to sight; therefore these [basic characteristics] of sight may be rediscovered in each individual form of art which has emanated therefrom: in architecture (1) pure proportions, (2) connection of arcs and straight lines, (3) the meaning of the whole; in sculpture (1) proportions of form, (2) anatomical truth, (3) connection of these in expression; in painting (1) proportion of light masses and shadow masses as well as spots of local color, (2) representation of space and of the objects in perspective view, (3) expression of the matter [here probably meaning texture] of objects as well as of the tone of the air [*sic*] (letter to Clemens Brentano, Dec. 5, 1809, *H.S.*I, pp. 187 ff.).

Runge consequently urges us to proceed from a unilateral to a multilateral approach to art, because our rational faculties urge us to do so and because the latter avenue will lead us to the "grandeur of existence." Runge seeks the synthesis in all things he approaches. As he seeks the identity of God and man, man and universe, universe and science, science and art, art and theory, theory and practice, so also does he search for the common denominator which will unite the arbitrarily divorced artistic disciplines in a school of art which will also function as a communal work-shop where all "scientific" work is directed toward making art theory into a philosophy of life and all practical work is channeled into the grand artistic production of the *Gesamtkunstwerk* in which the distinction between decorative and monumental art is fully dissolved.

Runge states:

All human endeavor which challenges the mind should ultimately lead us back to the highest spirit and be based upon it; otherwise it will be built on sand.

Now it is my solemn and holy will, to lead art back to the point, or found an art based on it, whereupon rests the foundation of the whole world. Whether this will be possible for me publicly and whether I shall be able to influence the public, I do not know, and I am willing to table that concern; but it is possible for me, if I continue to work on it with faithful diligence (letter to Pauline, 1801–1804, *H.S.*II, p. 177).

That it is this aspiration with which I identify my life as an artist is self-evident, and any lower concept must be distant from my soul. To bring into being a whole art epoch is God's concern and improper for us to try. Anyone who understands me is welcome, and as for the others, it does not help at all to even speak to them about it (letter to Daniel, Nov. 27, 1802, *H.S.*II, p. 170).

Thus Runge takes the most idealistic view of art possible for any man, one which equates aesthetics with the most noble ethical aspirations, one in which the practice of art becomes nearly a form of worship, a praise of God, and in which works of art become "heightened products of nature." Runge sees in his own ego and its creative impulse that spiritual agent which is commensurate with the "absolute ideal." Because he concentrates his main attention on the aesthetic function, it follows quite naturally that the work of art becomes for him the *modus vivendi et operandi* and the object of all human toil as well as the sharp focus which determines that creative release to which nature is subject "a priori." Runge believes that the artist does not merely copy nature in a work of art, but, as has been previously pointed out, that he produces nature consciously, just as nature itself produces itself unconsciously.

In a work of art, Runge saw the most perfect materialization of the ego to itself; that is, he considered it the conflux of subject and object, both being in effect identical, namely the ego itself. Therefore as the conscious (or rational human faculty) thus merges with the unconscious (or irrational natural faculty), it appeared to Runge that man provokes God Himself; after discussing at length his *Tageszeiten* and matters relating to theory, he exclaims: "There are moments in my life when a lightning strikes my soul, and I begin to realize what the right faith is, that of which Christ says it can move mountains. Oh! if I could only have it, reach it, express it so!—well, perhaps something beautiful might come of it, maybe in the last resort I am toying around with God's handiwork."

Runge's entire thinking on this subject parallels that of Schelling. But ultimately it goes back to the idea proposed by Kant, namely, that art is purposive within and purposeless without and therefore represents an autonomous universe which relates to man as the world relates to God (cf. letter to Daniel, May 16, 1803, *H.S.*II, p. 216). Paul Klee expresses the same idea for the twentieth century as follows:

His [the artist's] growth in his awareness and consideration of nature enables him to freely form abstract images which achieve for the work a new naturalness which goes beyond the pretentiously schematic. Then he creates works, or he participates in the creation of works, *which* are similes to the work of God [italics mine]. (Paul Klee, "Wege des Naturstudiums" in "Das Staatliche Bauhaus Weimar, 1919–23," in H. M. Wingler's *Das Bauhaus*.)

Intentionally, at the conclusion of this chapter and ostensibly for reasons of "completeness," it is necessary to take up a concern which, skirting the borders of both basic art theory and metaphysics, is most difficult to isolate as being either one or the other and is therefore not easy to discuss rationally. We already know that Runge was deeply indebted to Böhme and his mystical world allegory which draws freely from medieval numbers theory, alchemy, plane geometry, astronomy and astrology, as well as from neo-Platonic scales of essences within the fantastic infrastructure of the mystic's own invention; in short, that he was, at least superficially, familiar with the whole spectrum of Böhmian thought constructs which by themselves certainly constitute a separate and major topic of discussion. Inasmuch as traces of the teachings of Paracelsus, Tauler, Ficino, Pico, Bruno, and Luther converge in Böhme, the influences emanating from him and found in those whom he influenced are as varied as the rainbow. It is generally noted that Milton, Coleridge, and Blake as well as Runge drew on a common inspirational source in Böhme, and the last two mentioned particularly on the copper engravings which illustrate the seventeenth-century editions of the mystic's writings (p. 27). Runge's drawing for *Der Morgen* uses symbols and images derived from those plates. (Compare Chapter V.)

Because of countless allusions to the matter of mystical polarities, the Trinity, the Sacraments, mystic interpretations of nature and divinity, the Apocalypse of St. John, and others, biographers of Runge have found in the unraveling of his mysticism a major focus of interest. It is one, however, which is not patently suited to our goal—to assess concisely Runge's essential and lasting contributions to the theory of art. It is the contention of this discussion that, while the primacy of Runge's faith germane to his theory cannot be overstated, nevertheless the auxiliary mystical apparatus attending that faith need not be elevated to the same supremacy of rank for our purposes. At least three reasons prompt me to make such an

assumption. The importance which Runge attaches to mystogogy diminishes perceptively as he grows older. Runge's color theory points in its
later phases toward an increased departure from that interest. And even if
this were not so, we can continue reading Runge (after the initial shock!)
and separate, in our own minds, fact from mystery, when Runge speaks
and when Böhme, when we hear Runge the sober art theorist and when,
Runge the religious fanatic. Chapter V will of necessity involve substantial
portions of Runge's mystogogy in an effort to present the "flavor" of his
personal iconography. That section of our study will treat Runge's
personal artistic elaboration and symbolic distillation of his universal
theory. But at this point a few summary observations may suffice to suggest
that added dimension operative in the artist's thoughts and beliefs.

In a rather long letter to Daniel, Runge speaks first at length about
the "connection between mathematics, music and color" and how this connection can be expressed through images of "flowers, figures, and lines,"
and then he ruminates about the "truth of color," the "basic concepts of
faith," and his own "strength of faith." He further states that "the world
consists of tone and line, of color and drawing, of love and law, of inner
faith and external, i.e., civil or worldly relations; that it consists of the first
idea, of premonition and of love; that it is composed of the frame, of the
form [*Gestalt*] and the figures of the picture." Thereafter he remonstrates
with the powers that be, pleads with important literary figures, particularly
Tieck and the Schlegels, entreats imaginary personifications of good and
evil, which, according to Runge, exist in the world as astringent polarities
locked in irreconcilable, celestial combat in the universe and in history. He
continues thus (cf. *H.S.*I, pp. 36 ff.) :

Whoever has the right faith and searches with it the exterior world, that man will
find all science, because all emanates from the inner ray of light, that is, the living
breath, the picture of God in us, the Word, the beginning of all things; from it
have derived the colors, that is the One and the Three, that is, the Longing, the
Love and the Will, that is yellow, red and blue, the Point, the Line and the Circle,
muscles, blood and bones, that is, the unrest and the life of the world, as they move
in the eclipse, that is the time and the passion; the closer they move to the circle,
to the straight line, to the mathematical point, the ray of light, the closer they
move toward faith, innocence, childhood, the closer man and the world move toward perfection, peace and dispassion: that is eternity, the Kingdom of Heaven,
paradise.

Runge also provides us with a geometric figure consisting of six bisecting
circles, containing a triangle and a hexagon within, to explain his concept
graphically (*H.S.*I, p. 41).

We notice that Runge distinguishes between the "right faith" and the
knowledge that faith may effect in man. But inasmuch as Runge's personal
mystical insights born from that faith have as much universal validity as the

next man's it is futile to expand further on that "knowledge" as it would entail discoursing upon religious fantasizing in general, leaving the impression that one is chasing elusive phantoms. Conversely, the more narrowly artistic concern of point, line, and surface is of greater interest to us, for it leads us directly to the twentieth century and Kandinsky (cf. W. Kandinsky, *Punkt und Linie zu Fläche*, 1926). Runge says that it is impossible for man to express the "mathematical point" or the "mathematical line." Man cannot penetrate these with the senses but only with "cold mathematical reason." The "point," according to him, can appear to our imagination only at a brief instance, because at that point all thoughts cease to exist. Runge likens the "point" to the "Word of God" from which all things flow and to which they again return. All efforts to "imagine that line out of that point" are futile and "as far as the surface is concerned, that is the devil himself."

We have previously seen how Runge attempts to fuse the basic elements of the arts, and the arts with general science, and how these attempts were coupled with synesthesia. Now we hear again of these concerns in the expanded framework of mysticism:

Light and line divided into three, into mathematics, color and words; in music, lines, words and color flow together, they are the Will, the Love and the Longing united in faith; these are the pure components of Man as God first created him. Then, through the Fall of Man was brought into the world good and evil and through their mixture came the passions, inwardly good and wicked on the outside; anyone who understands the inner passions also understands the outer ones; nothing is pure, because the earth has been thrown out of the circle and into the ellipse (letter to Tieck, April 1803, *H.S.*I, p. 40).

May these few examples suffice. It becomes readily apparent how these and similar passages appearing all too often throughout *Hinterlassene Schriften* can throw the unwary reader completely off course. We must, therefore, always discriminate between Runge the dreaming, incomprehensible mystic-reveler and Runge the faithful, imaginative, diligent, comprehensible artist-theorist. Also, we should always differentiate between Runge's unique gifts of constructive creative fantasy and his (in large part) ruminating, eclectic, tropological phantasmagoria. As Runge's practically applicable and universally valid art theory derives from the former, and his personal iconography in large part from the latter, our separation of that iconological concern as an "appendix" to our study and as an introductory guide to Runge's own allegorical art is consistent with logic.

My major thesis here is (1) that Runge's theory and Runge's art should not be dealt with unitarily but rather that these two concerns require separate and special attention; and (2) that the content of *Hinterlassene*

Schriften should be divided into two distinct rubrics. *First,* there are those pronouncements which, if rationally evaluated, provide the general objective basis for a revolutionary new post-Baroque art theory or system of aesthetics and, as distinct from the classic, form the basis of the Christian-Romantic approach to art. They form the most ambitious and exhaustive document delineating Romanticism in art existing in literature. As such it is a timeless, universally valid monument to Romanticism and the spirit of man and not subject to critique based on Runge's art. *Second,* there are all those statements that bear witness to Runge's special and personal mystical, anagogical, tropological, zodiacal, physiognomic, pantheistic, nature-philosophical, and other such interests which collectively and in conjunction with the above provide the subjective basis for his personal iconography and symbolic art. They represent *one* man's first tentative and halting steps in an attempt to venture beyond the confines of the known and conventional into the vast unknown unlocked by the romanticism of his own invention. Runge's art, therefore, is naturally limited in time and place, and largely characteristic of the artist's period. It could even be dealt with out of context with Runge's theory, for no theory can really enhance the inherent legitimacy of a work of art. Both theory and practice must be able to stand on their own and be subject to independent evaluation.

If we choose this basic approach to the study of Runge as the *conditio sine qua non,* we will eliminate a great deal of that confusion which plagues so much of the Runge scholarship today. I propose then a methodology which distinguishes sharply between Runge's theory and his work, on the one hand, and, on the other, separates within the body of that theory that which is generally applicable. By "generally applicable," I refer to that which has universal relevancy to the collective spirit of probity in attitude, individualism in conduct, authenticity in expression, freedom in style, and experimentalism in technique generically characteristic of the significant phases and aspects of modern art, as distinguished from that which is only specifically material to Runge's personal iconography embodied in his symbolic art, or that which has limited significance as an art historical curio. Once we have made this distinction—chosen a heterogeneous classification rather than a homogeneous aggregate of critical priorities— we can come to a full understanding of Runge's achievement, free from the constant questions about the artist's concrete realization of his ideas, and, *mutatis mutandis,* clear of attempts, based on his art, at discrediting his ideas. Those questions and these attempts will then not only fade in meaning and become mere "academic" exercises, but, more importantly, what is now merely implied by innuendo will then clearly evolve, namely, that Runge's genius was paramount in ideology and not in creativity.

Moreover, this methodology of a consistent unilateral categorization of relevancies will relieve Runge's work from the yoke of his theory, and from those persistent doubts arising out of a multilateral agglomeration of tangents, as to what might have, could have, may have, or should have been if Runge had carried out all of his plans into practice. It will enable us to judge his work in accordance with factual evidence alone, in a manner unencumbered by all that which was "promised" by Runge to be "delivered," and we will see it for what it actually is and not what it might be on condition of the artist's good intentions and the wishful thinking of his biographers. If I am allowed to venture a prediction, four developments may probably then occur: (1) The now somewhat inflated over-all image of Runge's practical oeuvre, particularly with regard to his symbolic pictures, will diminish in exact ratio to the decrease in its presently exaggerated speculative involvement in Runge's problematical writings. (2) A reversal in the history of the Runge critique will take place and we will once again, as did those writers before World War I, justly recognize his major merits, contributions, and innovations in the areas of realism, naturalism, open air portraiture, plein-air landscape, and experimentation with color. (3) It will then, in spite of at least one most striking, even though unfinished realization—*Morning*, Large Version—become manifest that Runge's tentative assumptions and probing implications laid down in his hypotheses were not nearly exhausted by him in their empirical consequences, but, owing to the immense fecundity of their ramifications, required the practical activity and experimentation of many artists over many decades to be realized gradually and piecemeal. (4) Runge's place as theorist, aesthetician, critic, pedagogue, and visionary reformer, who laid the ideational basis for the modern approach to the practice of art, can then be evaluated precisely, meaningfully, and unconditionally, in its unique historical position and singular importance for our time.

IV. COLOR

*T*HE following brief discussion of Runge's theories on color in general, and of his publication entitled *Colorsphere* in particular, is a comprehensive introductory treatise intended to organize the overwhelming scope of Runge's far-flung theories on color into its important lines of thrust and to classify its implications into major topical areas with added endeavors at analysis and interpretation.

The full title of Runge's publication is *Colorsphere or the Construction of the Relationship of all Color Mixtures to each other and their complete Affinity; with an added Attempt of a Diversion concerning the Harmony of Color Compositions.* It was published by F. Perthes in Hamburg, in 1810 (*H.S.*I, pp. 112 ff.). This publication contains also a dissertation by Heinrich Steffens entitled *Über die Bedeutung der Farben in der Natur,* in which he amplifies and corroborates as physicist the artist's views (cf. Chapter III).

Because of technical limitations on my part, the purely mechanical considerations of Runge's color system in its relation to the physical properties of light will largely be omitted. But it will become apparent that such expertise in the science of physics in our context is neither necessary nor desirable. Most of his biographers treat Runge's color theory in a most cursory manner or omit it entirely from their discussions. While by no means exhaustive then, this study may prove to be of value as an introduction to Runge's color theory and as further illumination of his ability to combine "fiery Christian faith, ardent imagination and a profound investigative spirit" in the crucible of his genius, from the perspective of an added dimension (said by Perthes, quoted from Berefelt, *Philipp Otto Runge,* p. 15).

We have previously indicated Runge's ideas concerning the historical background necessitating the institution of a new science of color, and we have pointed out that Runge's color theory was intimately linked to his mystical world view, that he invested color with a spontaneous vitality and an immanent dynamism of its own—comparable to a mystical entelechy of color as causative agent in the form-giving processes in nature—and that he ascribed an importance to the study of color which was tantamount to the study of art itself. Large portions of his color theory transcend, because of Runge's mystical inscrutability, the bounds of logical inquiry. We will, in the present context, avoid as far as possible becoming involved in that mystogogy, and instead focus our attention on such parts of the theory as are accessible to rational analysis.

Daniel's statement concerning the inscrutability of parts of Runge's color theory helps to give perspective to the problem:

We encountered metaphysical difficulties for the solution of which neither I nor he [i.e., Runge] had the ability. However, I dare to predict how it would have come could we have enjoyed his vigorous presence longer. His straight eye would have furnished him real data concerning the deeper relationships and we could have, as on previous occasions, helped each other in the logical disentanglement of his pronouncements (Daniel's letter to Goethe, Oct. 13, 1811, *H.S.*II, p. 434).

Because we know that the project of the *Tageszeiten* cycle stood in the center of Runge's life from the end of the year 1802 until his death, it is important for us to know also what relationship existed in the artist's mind between that life's undertaking and the study of color. Runge writes: "During the summer [of 1804] I have continued to study the treatment of color and I have only thus arrived at the manner in which to finish the Tageszeiten completely" (letter to Tieck, March 29, 1805, *H.S.*I, p. 60). We might add that that was merely the beginning; all subsequent productions, particularly his portraits, should be regarded as preparatory studies in the treatment of color. The final "pay-off" and culmination of all these labors did not occur until the years 1808/9 when Runge began, with infinite care and caution, to apply what he had learned in the two color versions of the first plate of *Tageszeiten*, namely *Der Morgen*.

"It is my opinion that all knowledge and all art of man should never be anything else but to announce the praise of the highest God" (letter to Quistorp, Aug. 16, 1803, *H.S.*II, p. 234). Runge's general theoretical notions regarding, first, the understanding of science and art as a praise of God and, second, the idea of the absolute necessity for an artist to penetrate the secrets of nature and thus obtain the knowledge of the "instruments" upon which he plays before engaging in the practice of art, are not merely "idle words"; Runge subjects himself to the same disciplined approach and consequence of priorities. Runge says that "none will believe how necessary it is for the poor artist (and they don't even believe it) to base their talents on really clear scientific tasks, because the only reason for all the uncertainty is the fact that people do not even know the instruments upon which they are supposed to play" (cf. letters to Brentano, Dec. 5, 1809, *H.S.*I, pp. 189 ff., and to Schelling, Feb. 1, 1810, *H.S.* I, pp. 156 ff.). Thus the need for the systematic development of a color theory for use by artists stood at the forefront of Runge's thinking at all times. But he also writes "Color is the last art which is still mystical to us and must always remain so."

Let us briefly summarize Runge's mystical ideas concerning color. The three primary colors are the symbol of the Trinity, black (or darkness) and white (or light) symbolize evil and good; blue is the "Father," red the "Mediator," and yellow the "Consoler" (letter to Daniel, Nov. 7, 1802, *H.S.*I, p. 17). Born from our faith came the picture of God in our soul which in turn gave rise to colors—yellow ("longing"), red ("love"), and blue ("will") (letter to Daniel, March 23, 1803, *H.S.*I, p. 37). The paradise of the three pure colors is closed to us. But the light that came into the world became lost in the darkness of evil until Christ's death on the Cross gave it back to us in our faith (letter to Tieck, March 29, 1805, *H.S.*I, p. 60). Runge illustrates further with the help of a diagram his color symbolism: in a hexagon appear in the top corner red as "the ideal" and "love," and reading clockwise, blue and violet as "woman" and the "female passion," green as the "real," yellow and orange as "man" and the "male passion" (*H.S.*I, p. 264).

I am becoming increasingly more convinced, the clearer the form of the new optics for painting appears to me, how it lies within the nature of seeing itself that art has declined so far and has even perished and by necessity will continue to do so before a better and mightier art comes along (letter to Klinkowström, Sept. 1, 1809, *H.S.*I, p. 177).

As we have seen previously, Runge ascribes the "decline of art" in general to a decline in the knowledge of color, of which, he claims, Correggio and certain of the Dutch masters had an intuitive understanding— one, however, that was not sufficiently entrenched in their practical methodology as to affect succeeding generations.

Since Leonardo da Vinci and before him attempts had been made to lend the treatment of colors in painting a support by means of a solid scientific basis concerning the color in nature; and through the astounding discoveries and efforts of artists as well as scholars, chiefly Newton, it has become impossible to rely in this matter any longer merely on one's feelings. The doctrine of the fraction of light rays has now provided the painters with a presumed insight into these natural phenomena, but has also only increased the fear of the insurmountability of the media. This doctrine merely penetrated into the knowledge of the painters but left them even more helpless in the practical application and it is now becoming impossible to become free again unless we work our way through with the most definite clarity (1806 [?], *H.S.*I, p. 75).

It appears, therefore, that Runge distinguished at all times between the theoretical, scientific study of light as belonging to the domain of physics, and the practical study of color as pigments for use by artists. It is therefore wrong to embroil Runge in the Goethe-Newton controversy which concerned a fundamental disagreement on the properties of white light as containing the prism colors and being made up of them, Goethe choosing the explanation of white light that transcends its mere composition of the prism colors. (For an astute discussion of Goethe's scientific fiasco, see Charles Sherrington, *Goethe on Nature and on Science*.) Runge, unlike Goethe, had no quarrel with Newton at all; both men are merely concerned with different aspects of color, that is, as physical light and as pigments on the palette. Daniel substantiates this view by means of the "expert opinions" of such men as Görres, Steffens, T. Mayer, Lambert, and others (*H.S.*II, pp. 506 ff.; *H.S.*I, p. 170; cf. "Aus den Nordischen Miscellen, Hamburg, 1810, No. 9 vom 4. März: Über die Farbenkugel des Mahlers P. O. Runge; von einem Freunde des Verfassers," *H.S.*II, pp. 543 ff.).

Schopenhauer saw the full significance of this "theoretical battle of the century" when he commented about it in "Die Welt als Wille und Vorstellung" (*Sämtliche Werke* I, p. 257). The following illuminating passage illustrates the fervor of the debate and, even more, the magnitude of an error that can be committed by the greatest of poetic-philosophical minds:

Goethe has been sufficiently blamed by the uncomprehending opponents of his color theory for a lack of mathematical knowledge: of course, here, where it does not matter to calculate and measure according to hypothetical data, but rather where it depends on the direct cognition of the mind with regard to the causes and effects, that reproach was so completely uncalled for and out of place that those doing the reproaching have demonstrated by their action, as much as by their other Midas-pronouncements, their total lack of power of judgment. The fact that today, nearly half a century after the publication of Goethe's color theory, and even in Germany, the Newtonian taradiddles still remain undisturbed in the possession of academic chairs and that one continues quite seriously to talk of the seven homogeneous lights and their variable refractions,—that fact will one day be counted among the great intellectual characteristics of humanity in general and of Germany in particular.

Runge's essential distinction of the study of light as science and of color as artistic theory is of great importance for us, and of even greater practical value for the studio artist because it simplifies and narrows down the problem for him considerably. Runge assures us that the colors of which one generally speaks (i.e., the physical colors in nature) are something quite different from those which we can use in painting (letter to Tieck, March 29, 1805, *H.S.*I, p. 60). Yet Runge's intentions are not always understood in their unequivocal meaning by his biographers. One of the two studies about Runge in the English language, that by J. B. C. Grundy, states: "Runge seems well aware that white is not a color but a combination of colors, yet he disregards the Newtonian explanation and considers color as a separate manifestation, though he includes chiaroscuro in his treatment of the subject" (*Tieck and Runge, A Study in the Relationship of Literature and Art in the Romantic Period with Special Reference to "Franz Sternbald,"* p. 82). Runge does not "disregard" the Newtonian "explanation" but with good reason does not find it helpful for his task. The clause containing the word "chiaroscuro" in Grundy's statement seems to bear no thematic relationship to the rest of the sentence. Grundy's study, incidentally, lists the following five "original factors of Runge's work": arabesque, color, technique, subject, and the fusion of the arts. He uses the term "technique" to denote such elements as "foreground flowers, use of frames, use of landscapes," etc. Thus he obviously confuses the term technique with style. Grundy immediately apologizes for his five qualifications as being more or less meaningless!

In addition to proposing a methodology in the use of pigments for artists, Runge points our attention, as already noted, to a most startling property of color, namely, that which falls into the province of psychology and man's ability to experience color in an "unconsciously symbolic" manner. In an important letter written in 1810 to Goethe, to whom Runge had previously sent a copy of his recently published *Colorsphere*, Runge states the problem of "psychological color":

It is impossible to expect a sure method and doctrine for the practical treatment of color in painting unless we first conceive of the total effects in nature as if they were pictures or paintings in which we can render that treatment in correspondence with their [the pictures'] meaning. Then a lot will happen by itself, especially if a general understanding of the relationship between light and matter through the intermediation of colors becomes possible. Then the colors on our palette will have the same meaning, and what artist will be able to bear it that the use of colors stands in contradiction with that which he recognizes in them as a condition of nature and of pigment? (letter to Goethe, Feb. 1, 1810, *H.S.*I, pp. 180 ff.; cf. p. 111).

Let us restate Runge's proposition. Inasmuch as he sought for the synthesis of everything else, so also did he approach the study of color with such an astounding amount of thoroughness as to ponder the possibility of a "super color theory" which would encompass and give a common denominator to the following concerns: (1) the empirical, synthetic study of optical effects directly from observation of natural phenomena for purposes of their naturalistic representation with pigments upon the canvas; (2) the inductive study of colors as symbols of observable natural phenomena; (3) the deductive study of "psychological color" or of colors as symbols of psychic phenomena; (4) the ontological study of color as allegory of the nonobservable forces of nature presumed to be operative in it according to the antimistic-vitalistic-pantheistic-romantic nature philosophy; (5) the metaphysical study of color as metaphor of creation, God, the Trinity, the Old and New Testaments, in short, as allegory of the whole mystogogical thought construct emanating from Runge's religious, mystico-anagogical world view.

It may be added to point 1 that this part of Runge's inquiry produced perhaps the most impressive practical results especially in Runge's plein-air portraiture and landscapes. That this method of investigation and desire for heightened realism and "naturalism" leads us directly to the Barbizon School and Impressionism has been noted and stressed by the early Runge scholarship, which saw in Runge's "plein-airism" and veduta a direct fore-runner of Impressionism (cf. Gustav Pauli, *Philipp Otto Runges Zeichnungen*, p. 17): "It is correct to say that Runge's art contained the seed of an element which was later to bloom in the naturalism and Impressionism of the nineteenth century." That opinion is based, no doubt, on such elements in Runge's paintings as, for example, the Elbe estuary views appearing in *Der Grosse Morgen* (Hamburg Kunsthalle, inv. no. 1022) and the harbor scene in *Das Bild der Eltern* (Hamburg Kunsthalle, inv. no. 1001); more-over, the realistic veduta of the Lower-Saxonian country milieu appearing in the background of *Die Hülsenbeckschen Kinder* (Hamburg Kunsthalle, inv. no. 1012). Not least of all, here must be mentioned a little flower study (*Amaryllis*, Hamburg Kunsthalle, inv. no. 2032) done in rich, spontaneous, masterly *alla prima* strokes which is so startling in its effect of "modernity," its disposition of values, its sketchy description of form as to put it some seventy years ahead of its time.

Point 2, it seems, leads us to Expressionism and the art of a Van Gogh, the Symbolism of a Gauguin, both artists having had an extensive awareness of colors as symbol bearers. Point 3 leads us again to Van Gogh and Gauguin, but particularly to the Nabis, Synthetism, Symbolism, and ultimately to Abstract Expressionism (cf. Chapter II and also page 57). (For two brilliant discussions of Romantic art theories as foundation for modern abstract art, consult Otto Stelzer, *Die Vorgeschichte der abstrakten Kunst, Denkmodelle und Vorbilder*, and K. Lankheit, *Die Frühromantik und die Grundlagen der gegenstandslosen Malerei*.)

For an excellent discussion of problems relating to color in art generally and in particular of Runge's achievement of an "effective transcendental light" in his paintings of *Der Morgen*, see Wolfgang Schöne, *Über das Licht in der Malerei*. Schöne states (p. 215) that Runge can be credited with the "most difficult to comprehend but also the most distinct, and if we understand it, the most comprehensive statement about light, produced in the early nineteenth century."

Runge divides the problem of his color investigation into the follow-ing categories and groupings: (1) points 1–4: hues, values, and chromas.

(2) points 5–8: matter, texture, transparency, opacity. (3) points 9–12: metaphysical relationships. (4) mystical-anagogical relationships (cf. "Rubrics to the Dissertation," *H.S.*I, p. 162). Runge's contribution in section 4 above, of course, lies at the core of his new Romantic-Christian art and as such figures most importantly in helping replace the bankrupt realism and naturalism of Baroque art with the vigorous spiritualism and expressionism of airy abstractions. It is significant for us that the decisive threshold of this transition to "modern art" lies (and not only for Runge) in the changing attitude toward color in the nineteenth century and an investment of that element of form with an importance and meanings going beyond anything seen in history. I believe that a thorough analysis of these changing ideas about color occurring during the nineteenth century goes the longest way toward a full understanding of that art historical period.

Depending on whether one roots for Impressionism or Expressionism (in all its many forms), one will either see Runge's chief contribution in point 1 or points 2 through 5, respectively. If we consider for a while that Runge had a similarly all-inclusive notion about the other elements of form besides color—about line, texture, value, and shape—and that he attempted to encompass all of these ideas into four paintings (*Tageszeiten*), and if we add to this his ideas of the "total work of art" which was to comprise all the artistic media with their corresponding elements of form interpreted according to the five points listed above in context with a "super color theory," it becomes readily apparent that only a divine power (or an IBM computer) could ever hope to transform precept into action. We can only recall at this point what Goethe said about the *Tageszeiten* and Runge: "Look at that stuff, what devil's work, and here again, what charm and magnificence the lad produced; but after all, the poor devil could not bear it, he is already gone; it would not be possible otherwise: anyone who stands on the verge in this manner, must die or go crazy, there is no grace" (Maltzahn, *Philipp Otto Runge's Briefwechsel mit Goethe*, p. 117). This passage was recorded by Sulpiz Boisserée after a visit with Goethe and an inspection of his "Runge room" which contained a number of the artist's drawings and silhouettes, on March 2, 1811, a few months after Runge's death. Of course, Goethe would never have spoken as candidly in any of his own numerous written statements about Runge. If Sulpiz Boisserée were not generally considered to be a reliable informant, we might have some doubts about the authenticity of that statement.

Runge was by no means an amateur in the study of color. He was well acquainted with, or built upon, the views and publications of many important contributors to the field, either through study or personal conversation and correspondence with them. Thus he knew the leading arguments proposed by Leonardo, Dürer, Newton, Goethe, Mengs, Casanova, J.H.W. Tischbein, Oken, Eich, Steffens, and such early epistemological-ontological sources as Böhme, Swedenborg, Harsdörfer, and many more (cf. letters to Klinkowström, Feb. 24, 1809, *H.S.*I, pp. 172 ff.; to his brother Karl, April 16, 1810, *H.S.*I, pp. 183 ff.; to Daniel, Jan. 16, 1803, *H.S.*II, pp. 193 ff.). Runge's correspondence with Goethe dealt almost exclusively with matters relating to color; that with the scientist H. Steffens, in large part. Steffens writes: "What Albrecht Dürer and, above all, Leonardo da Vinci had written about color was very well known to him" (*Was Ich Erlebte*, p. 213).

There can be no doubt that Runge's invention of the "color sphere" as model to illustrate the relationship of all color mixtures (i.e., mixture ratios) to each other represents his most important practical contribution in the field, one which enriches it also in a lasting manner. These color mixture ratios include all their respective hues (the distinction between one color and another), values (the range of greys from white to black), and chromas (the resultant mixtures of hues and values) in such a way as to demonstrate, in the model of the sphere, all possible nuances of color at a glance.

The "color sphere" as model can be visualized as the earth globe: through its center runs the north-south axis or value column from white through the greys to black. The hues appear along the equator, the chromas in the spheric sections between the equator and the poles, and "pure grey" appears in the mathematical center of the sphere. The sphere is identical to the Munsell system, currently in wide usage, in all significant aspects, as far as I can determine. (For critiques of the *Colorsphere* by Steffens, Brentano, Örtzen, and Goethe compare *H.S.*II, pp. 387, 388, 404, 410, 541, and 542. For contemporary periodical reviews see *H.S.*II, pp. 543 ff.) Runge arrived at this impressive result through years of patient empirical research and observation, and the model itself is of substantial practical use for the studio practitioner of today. How does Runge answer the question what the "color sphere" is? "It is not a work of art but a mathematical figure of a few philosophical reflections" (letter to his brother Gustaf, Nov. 22, 1808, *H.S.*II, p. 372).

The "color sphere" is not reproduced in *Hinterlassene Schriften* because of printing difficulties of the color nuances appearing on the original plates. Compare in this regard also Daniel's footnote entry (*H.S.*I, p. 112) which justifies the omission for reasons of sufficient textual clarity and comprehensibility without the model, which is rather a strange argument indeed. Aubert says: "Brücke [in his *Physiologie der Farben für die Zwecke der Kunstgewerbe*] thinks that the incomplete reproduction of the color sphere in Runge's disputation can be explained in essence by the factory like Coloring process. [A most reasonable assumption.] And he does so with full right, because Runge's original leaves which are now located in the Kunsthalle at Hamburg are a marvel of coloristic sensitivity" (*Runge* *und die Romantik*, p. 102). I must heartily concur in that view, for my own inspection of the watercolor plates in the *Kupferstichkabinett* of the Hamburg Kunsthalle has also convinced me of Runge's extraordinary sensitivity to the finest shadings, gradings, subtleties, and nuances of color. A recent publication (1959) makes available for the first time a foldout color plate of Runge's watercolor studies to the *Farbenkugel* (*Ph. O. Runge, Die Farbenkugel und andere Schriften zur Farbenlehre*). This little volume contains the most important theoretical writings on color by Runge and an epilogue by J. Hebing.

In the nearly one hundred pages in *Hinterlassene Schriften* devoted entirely to Runge's color theories, several other essays and theses appear alongside the dissertation on the *Colorsphere* (cf. *H.S.*I, pp. 84 ff.). Let us briefly name the most important of these and give abstracts of them in the order of their appearance. "The Elements of Color" is a discourse on the relationship of art to nature and how the former vies with the latter with regard to their identical basic creative elements. From this contention arises the need of studying artists' media in context with study of the media of nature. (We have already discussed how these findings led Runge to accept the same idealistic results—that art is a second nature—as those at which Schelling arrived.) Runge says there are only three colors plus white and black, and from the mixture of these five basic parts (white, black, red, yellow, and blue) all the other colors result. A table or "total mixability chart" of 11 different rubrics listing the pure colors (3), black and white (2), the pure mixtures of the three primaries (3, i.e., orange, violet, and green), pure grey (1), and 5 more mixing options of all the above, results in 3,405 different hues, values, and chromas including black and white. It is quite clear that this is an arbitrary figure: although Runge's approach is quite correct, the actual figure, if such a one can be ascertained at all, is infinitely larger. But at one point Runge also suggests that there may be an infinite number of mixtures. (See "Über Zusammenstellung in Beziehung auf Harmonie. Fragmente," *H.S.*I, p. 132.)

A letter to Goethe, reproduced also in Goethe's *Farbenlehre* (*H.S.*I, pp. 88 ff.), contains much of the above material, considerably expanded, refined, and elaborated. In addition, Runge approaches here the problem of the opacity and translucency of textures and natural objects, relates these to their respective reproductive pigments (opaque and transparent colors), and thus brings considerable order to a most vexing studio problem. The problem of brilliant and translucent as opposed to vitiated and opaque colors is discussed by Runge with a keen knowledge of the *velare* and body color systems, toning, *sfumato*, and so forth.

Two more long letters follow in which the discussion is broadened to include a comparison of Runge's six-color system (red, yellow, blue, orange, green, and violet) with Newton's seven-color system (the six named plus indigo), while paying tribute to the Englishman's scientific genius. But Runge adds that he does not collide with Newton on the issue of the seven prismatic colors, because his color circle (which is the equator of the color sphere) provides also for indigo and magenta (the Newtonian equivalent of Runge's violet) by virtue of his splitting violet into a blue and red sector, which distinction he also included in the total mixability chart. This can also be compared with the corresponding color studies (at the Hamburg Kunsthalle) in which the breakdown into seven colors, including indigo and magenta in the Newtonian sense, is clearly rendered for all to see.

Runge states that the phenomenon of the fraction of white light into the colors of the prism (and their reconstitution into white light), Newton's chief discovery, does not help the artist at all but rather only tends to confuse him. Thus again, Runge draws a sharp dividing line between the science of physics and the "science of the studio." He further states that the consistency of objects determines chroma and that the mixed palette results in "pure grey" (which appears at the exact center of the color sphere or in the very middle of the north-south axis or value column) and not white as one would be led to believe after studying Newton. Runge is of course right, as no one has ever succeeded in mixing a "batch of white" from the pure colors on the palette in the studio after finding himself depleted in his supply of zinc or lead!

The *Farbenkugel*, which follows, contains all of the above findings summarized: a recapitulation of the distinction of physical colors and pigments; the model of the "color sphere"; eight auxiliary geometric visual aids, which, if assembled in superimposition, result in the complex "color sphere"; a re-emphasis of the compatibility of Newton's septagonal with his hexagonal color wheel; and a compelling defense of the "color sphere" as the only geometric model permitting the viewer to perceive the total range of hues, values, and chromas and their aggregate spectrum of mixability options at a glance. That model has lost nothing of its efficacy as a visual aid tool in studio instruction, and by putting all the elements of color into their proper relationship to each other it retains its full validity to this day.

Several more long essays follow. One of particular interest for us is "an attempt to rhyme the sensual impressions of the combinations of the different colors with the previously developed schema" (*H.S.*I, pp. 123 ff.), for in it Runge presents to us in effect some of the cardinal points of departure of the Impressionistic color method. In twenty-nine paragraphs, Runge develops the essential points of divisionism, optical mixture, juxtaposition of complementaries, and simultaneity of contrasts which, while startling in and by themselves as a new departure in color theory, also found their way into Runge's paintings, which pioneered in the field of plein-air portraiture, naturalistic veduta, and the rendering of light and atmospheric effects, particularly those of the times of the day. The latter fact, of course, explains the tendency among Runge's earlier biographers, who themselves were raised in the Impressionist tradition of visual perception and were thus especially inclined to appreciate its historical forerunners, to classify Runge's oeuvre as proto-Impressionistic.

Because Runge obviously does not change, but the times in which his biographers live do, it does not surprise us to see that more recent writers opt for their current stylistic trends as Runge's spiritual progenies. What is startling, however, to a considerable degree, is what J. M. Speckter writes in the *Nieder-Elbische Merkur* of 1815 about Runge: "In his own artistic development it had become clear and certain to him that since the apogee of the Greeks the art of forms in its correctness and strength as well as in the life and beauty of contours had been nearly exhausted by the Florentines and Raphael, that it had been completed and brought close to perfection,—but that, conversely, *light, color and moving life*, although deeply felt by many, . . . even clearly perceived, recognized and seized by Correggio and some others, had until now not been, to any significant extent, expressed by anyone as pure knowledge in word and law, in speech and deed" (italics mine; *H.S.*II, p. *526*). Thus a contemporary and friend of Runge characterizes the artist's theoretical endeavor with phrases that go begging as most worthy appendage to the Impressionist's method, some sixty years before Impressionism!

Another essay deserving undivided attention is "Concerning the basis of Harmony and Disharmony," in which Runge probes deeply into the nature of harmonious, disharmonious, and monotonous color combinations, thereby providing the contemporary studio practitioner with a fine guide to effective color grouping on the palette such as are commensurate with the results he desires (*H.S.*I, pp. *133* ff.). We have previously discussed Runge's concluding essay entitled "A Conversation about the Analogy of Color and Tones" in context with the artist's traits of synesthesia (cf. Chapter III; *H.S.*I, pp. *168* ff.).

The immense wealth of ideas on color contained throughout *Hinterlassene Schriften* and Runge's specific and technical disquisitions on color have not received the recognition which they deserve. This is in large part attributable to the scant interest in studio practice professed by art historians. Taken collectively, however, Runge's color theories represent a fully developed artist's handbook for the use of pigments and the effects obtainable through their methodical comprehension and application. I can only hope that this brief chapter, which has touched merely upon the most requisite of Runge's theorems, will incite those worthy of the undertaking and interested in artistic color theory to study Runge's contributions to that science in all their many implications and to make them available for use by present-day students of art.

V. ICONOGRAPHY

*A*T the end of Chapter III we pointed out that Runge's personal iconography, while lying well within the scope of our investigation of Runge's art theory, nevertheless represents a special concern that should properly be treated separately in a concluding appendage to our study. Runge's new symbolic art, being, no doubt, a most challenging artistic phenomenon, has stirred the minds of scholars for many decades, and the bulk of the literature dealing with Runge treats of that concern at great length. Despite all these efforts, however, and because of the uniquely arcane nature of Runge's symbolic art, it seems that the enigmatic interest it holds will not wane but will continue to occupy the imaginative faculties of art historians and aestheticians for many decades to come.

We know that Runge's first concern was "to have something to say," something that emanated from the "present moment of our existence with all its pains and pleasures"; how that was said was a subordinate problem to him (letter to F. W. J. Schelling, Feb. 1, 1810, *H.S.*I, p. 160). That basic Rungian and singularly romantic proposition concerning the priority of intention, desire, and plan over the attainment of the objective in final form in large measure contributed to the fragmentary and disjointed nature of the artist's oeuvre. As an attitude which is not infrequently found among German Romanticists it typifies the disconnected, incomplete, and inchoate state of some Romantic art and literature in that country. Nevertheless, Runge spent all of the years following his Dresden period until his death trying to find an appropriate "language" with which to express in visual images that which he considered worthwhile saying in the first place, in a manner and style that would be both contextually meaningful and formally clear and lucid. Because that personal subjective language of symbols which he invented and developed is so characteristic of Runge's philosophy of art, because it represents *one* specific possibility of a "new art" based on Runge's general romantic ideals and because, in a way, it amplifies for us much that has preceded this in our discussion, we may consider the following on the order of both a concluding expansion of our study as well as an introduction to Runge's allegorical landscape art.

We have seen that according to Runge's critical awareness the "historical composition" had run its course and anthropomorphic symbolism had become meaningless; conversely, the future for him pointed toward an animistic allegory of existence in a new art of "landscape painting" (Chapter III). If we add to this his keen interest in the investigation of natural phenomena, light, color, and his practice of plein-air painting, we might be quite naturally led to assume that this future of art merely held that promise for him toward which, some two decades later, the members of the Barbizon School labored so enthusiastically. But these men had in effect acquiesced in surrendering their right as artists to participate in the intellectual dialogue of their epoch by reducing their professional stature from that of spiritual leaders and commentators on the human drama to that of mere observers of nature, had thus become detached, passive, and objective reporters—the absence of profound compositional and stimulating symbolical efforts on their part indicating this "abdication." Runge, on the other hand, was not at all inclined toward compromising the highest humanistic-Christian ideals with which he invested the artistic calling, despite a pronounced affinity with the realistic and naturalistic method and style. Rather, Runge struck out in a different direction entirely, one that amounts to the most ambitious, complex, sophisticated, new Romantic iconography since the demise of the Christian-pagan world allegory of Renaissance art which it proposed to replace.

Starting off with a denunciation of the neoclassical "tittle-tattle" of Weimar, Runge suggests the necessity of the extinction of "all these corrupt newer works of art" as the necessary first step in the direction of a "growing, rather beautiful art, which is the landscape" (letter to Daniel, March 9, 1802, *H.S.I*, p. 14). He continues:

Is it not peculiar that we perceive our whole life clearly and distinctly when we see thick clouds, now reaching past the moon, now their edges gilded by the moon, now completely devouring the moon? It seems to us as if we could write our whole life's story in such pictures; and is it not true that no history painters, properly speaking, have lived since Raphael and Buonarroti? Even Raphael's picture here in the gallery [Sistine Madonna] leads straight toward landscape,— of course we must understand something entirely different when we speak of landscape (ibid., p. 15).

And indeed we must. To state it in the briefest possible form, we must understand the Rungian "landscape" neither as a realistic veduta, "views," or "prospects." Nor can we in any way associate its peculiar genre with the classic "ideal" or "heroic" landscape extravaganzas with accessory figures; nor, indeed, must we confound its kind with any landscape style that has preceded historically. (A certain, although highly tentative relationship exists between it and what Kenneth Clark in *Landscape into Art* prefers to call the "landscape of symbols" existing in the Middle Ages.) Rather it must be viewed as a feeling, an abstract, an essence of landscape, or, more specifically of nature, life, and divinity.

It appears to Runge that, historically, the multiplicity of symbols gave way to a progressive reduction of their number; while primitive cultures still worshipped "each individual spring, tree, rock, fire, and so on, Christian religion [Runge means Catholic religion] still required four persons to make up divinity, including the Holy Virgin and all the saints," a fact which seemed to Runge particularly conducive to foster the multi-figural historical composition. "The Reformation," Runge goes on to say, "limited itself to three persons in the image of divinity, that [latter image] seems to be perishing presently; the spirit of this religion was more abstract, but in no measure less fervent; out of it must also emanate a more abstract art" (ibid.). Runge never alludes to the nonhistorical (or non-historied) art of the Middle Ages, as, for example, iconic and devotional imagery which existed alongside the historical compositions (e.g., *Schmerzensmann, Erbärmdebild,* and other *Andachtsbild* variants, or Madonna Humilitatis, Lactans, della Misericordia, etc.). Either he had insufficient knowledge of it or he may have (quite aptly) attributed to such concrete visualizations of divinity an even larger measure of idolatrous portent than he did to historied representations.

At the root of Runge's new symbolic-pictorial language stands his invention of the child figure, the flower, and the child figure-flower composite symbols. Runge explains,

The pleasure which we experience in flowers, that really still originates in Paradise. Thus we connect inwardly always a meaning with the flower, therefore a human figure, and that [composite] only is the true flower which we have in mind in our joy. When we thus perceive in all of nature only our life, it is clear that only then can the true landscape come about in complete opposition to the human or historical composition.

And the world of colors, of which Runge said that it is "the last art which will always remain mystical to us," will become comprehensible to us again "only in the flower and in a wondrously enchanted way" (letter to Daniel, Nov. 7, 1802, *H.S.*I, p. 17). H. Börensen, in "Der Morgen von Ph. O. Runge . . .," interprets Runge's intention as follows: It is of the essence that we recognize that the intrinsic and original nature of man is revealed in the objects of nature. The art of landscape should not express any occasional feelings but should designate the innermost essence of man. Thus landscape art in the Rungian sense means a very real conquest over the opposition which separates man from nature, or, even more comprehensively, it represents the neutralization of the schism between spirit and matter.

According to Runge, people would slowly and in due time get used to the idea of always associating a given figure with a specific flower species in their minds, when viewing the new landscape paintings, and eventually it would not be necessary even to add the painted figures (letter to Tieck, Dec. 1, 1802, *H.S.*I, p. 27).

Runge's notion of a "flower language" is based on the assumption that the associative meanings accompanying the dialectic, regional, colloquial, or national usage of flower names represent a universal constant and therefore the basis for a generally comprehensible hieroglyphic idiom. Runge spent his childhood in the country and was familiar with most of its native vegetation, as witness his countless drawings and silhouettes of flowers and plants. A person brought up in the city may not be as conversant with flowers. Even a student of botany may encounter difficulties understanding Runge's flower language if he knows only the Latin terms of flowers but not Runge's native nomenclature. Compare in this regard L. Tieck who says: "The bitter juice which drips from the aloe, the Rittersporn [i.e. literally translated knight's spur; English: larkspur] which is named so in German by accident, cannot by itself in a picture suggest impenitence or bravery and courage. Thus there is much in these leaves [*Tageszeiten*] that only Runge himself understands and there is the danger that, owing to his compellingly rich fantasy he may fall ever deeper into the realm of arbitrariness and thereby neglect the form itself too much" (Ludwig Tieck, Eine Sommerreise, *Taschenbuch Urania für 1834*; cf. *H.S.* II, p. 539). If we add to this critique that of Friedrich Schlegel (cf. Chapter III) we might conclude that Runge's flower iconography was considered to be doomed to failure as a viable new language right from the start. It is in large part our intention in this chapter to demonstrate that these two men did not err in their judgments.

Runge expanded the flower language, at least in theory, to encompass also other "natural elements." "I am also thinking," he reflects, "of a picture in which we can give form and meaning to air, rocks, water and fire. In this manner, and we cannot realize that as yet, the landscape could develop out of this art and become a more lasting and magnificent art. You should not make images of God, because you are not able to do so. God cannot be comprehended by the human mind and He cannot be represented by any work of art" (letter to Daniel, Nov. 27, 1802, *H.S.*I, p. 21). Air, water, and fire!—the "free forms," abstract, nonobjective and non-descriptive by their very nature. We are, of course, immediately reminded of Turner who actually produced such ephemeral sights on his canvas. The saying "bilde Künstler, rede nicht" ("artist: form, do not talk!") seems a worthy aphoristic appendage here.

100

THE CHILDREN OF THE ARTIST, OTTO SIGISMUND AND MARIA DOROTHEA

1808/1809, oil on canvas, unfinished
38×50 cm.
H. K. Inv. No. 1026

MORNING (Large Version)

1809, oil on canvas, unfinished, reconstructed from nine fragments
151×111.5 cm.
H. K. Inv. No. 1022

LIGHT LILY AND MORNING STAR (Study for MORNING, Large Version)

1809, pen and ink
60.8 × 44.5 cm.
H. K. Inv. No. 34200

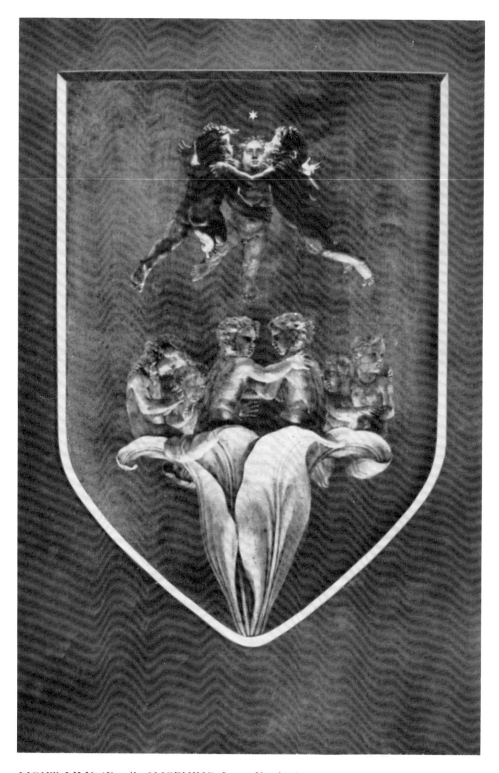

LIGHT LILY (Detail of MORNING, Large Version)

THE CHILD ON THE MEADOW (Detail of MORNING, Large Version)

MORNING (Large Version) (Detail)

FEMALE ROSE GENIE (Study for MORNING, Large Version)

1809, pencil and pen and ink
45.6× 36 cm.
H. K. Inv. No. 34197

WIFE OF THE ARTIST

1810, oil on canvas
49.5×39.5 cm.
H. K. Inv. No. 1013

Iconography

It can be seen that Runge's approach to abstraction as one based on a non-anthropomorphic romantic animism was very cautious and was to have been conducted in several successive stages because of Runge's apprehension "that other people might not be able to understand it." Nevertheless, it appears that Runge did lay the potential foundation of Expressionism when he stated that art should originate in the "present moment of existence with all its pains and pleasures," as he also prepared the theoretical basis for nonobjective abstract art in his color theory as well as in his notion of the reciprocal congruity which he saw in the meanings of flowers and colors. The flower and the flower-figure composite symbols therefore seem to have arisen in Runge's mind prompted by his desire to educate the people in successive stages in their ability to empathize with a fundamentally new artistic product, one based on the emotive qualities of natural phenomena. His was a didactic process which was eventually to have led to the ultimate goal, namely the psychological experiencing of abstract color patterns out of context with the conventional, object-related, descriptive, or qualifying function of color. That course proposed by Runge was to have availed itself of the "elements of landscape," rocks, and flowers in equal measure with water and fire, rushing clouds, and sunset skies, and even, surprising though this may sound—pure air—as building blocks for abstract and symbolical configurations that would result in powerful cryptograms expressing the psychic tremors of the artist, as much as they would move and stir the spectator in sympathetic emotional vibrations.

The starting points in Runge's formation and development of his new symbolic art were the two pictures entitled *Die Quelle und der Dichter* (*The Source and the Poet*) and *Die Mutter an der Quelle* (*The Mother at the Source*). (*Die Quelle und der Dichter*, 1805, pen and ink, 50.4 × 67 cm., Hamburg Kunsthalle, inv. no. 34257. *Die Mutter an der Quelle*, 1805 (?), oil on canvas, 62.5 × 78.1 cm., Hamburg Kunsthalle, inv. no. 1010.) The last-mentioned painting was loaned to an exhibition in Munich in 1931 where it was destroyed by fire. It is obvious that, in our context, we shall be able to discuss only a few, though very important, representative examples of Runge's many allegorical productions. It is my opinion that Daniel Runge's compendious description and interpretation of Runge's oeuvre (Zweites Buch, "Entwürfe zu Bildern," *H.S.*I, pp. 215–370) represents the most influential single attempt at ordering the artist's work into general stylistic categories, iconographic rubrics, and over-all artistic merit. In principle most writers concur in his views, as, for example, Isermeyer who says: "... it seems to me that in [Runge's] fragmented oeuvre his major work [*Tageszeiten*] is buried under his minor efforts" (*Ph. Otto Runge*, p. 44): he thus attributes the same paramount critical importance to *Tageszeiten* as does Daniel. Böttcher, whose main interest lies chiefly in Runge's contribution to portraiture, emphatically does not agree with Daniel. "In

Hinterlassene Schriften his brother attempted a listing of the works in groups that completely destroy the line of development because the portraits are treated by him as a mere appendage" (Böttcher, *Ph. O. Runge,* p. 283). It may be added that Runge himself considered portraiture a mere "appendage" to his life's undertaking and a "finger exercise" for his allegorical productions, even though the final historical verdict may still pronounce those "finger exercises" his finest contribution to art.

Runge says of *Die Mutter an der Quelle* that "the picture will be a source in the broadest sense of the word; also the source of all pictures which I will ever make, the foundation of the new art which I have in mind, also a spring in and by itself" (letter to Daniel, Nov. 27, 1802, *H.S.*I, p. 19). In context with Runge's early symbolic statements we should regard his "supra porta" *Triumph des Amor* as a significant first practical step toward the realization of the artist's theories (1801/02, oil on canvas, 66 × 173 cm., Hamburg Kunsthalle, inv. no. 2691). In this early painting Runge succeeds in weaving symbolically the whole story of the "stages of love" in life, from early youth to old age, into a single allegorical composition consisting of eighteen child figures in seven groupings, without the benefit of flowers. The "reading" of the whole configuration in its complex interrelationships requires both great sophistication and a keen sense of empathy on the part of the spectator so that he may perceive the work in keeping with Runge's painstaking intentions. Runge also furnishes us with a complete "program" for the picture (cf. *H.S.*I, pp. 218 ff.).

In a long poetic description of *Die Quelle und der Dichter,* the artist likens the water bubbles to flowers, the flowers to musical tones, the musical tones to colors; children ride the water bubbles and fade and disappear into the reeds. The earth is likened to a human being that is being formed as the "embryo is formed from the egg." In the center of the earth resides "the poor soul which longs for the light, just as we long for it." And when the "great birth of the world takes place, then will it be redeemed" (ibid, p. 20). It is to be noted that in this picture Runge's figure-flower composite symbol also appears fully developed for the first time. Runge says of it:

The nymph lies at the fountain and plays with her fingers in the water and the bubbles spring up large and the merry lads sit in the bubbles and want to come out, and as the bubbles burst they fly into the flowers and trees; the characters of the boys are in complete conformity with the flowers to which they belong, so that they give us a downright corporeal concept of the flowers. The lily stands in the highest light and the oak spreads as a hero its branches above them; . . . each individual flower always has a human character (*H.S.*I, pp. 200–21).

A tentative similarity between Runge and C. D. Friedrich can be reasonably suggested but only on the strength of these two compositions in which the "mood," just as in Friedrich's pictures, depends on the pictorial realities of naturalistically and not abstractly conceived landscape elements. That mood of reverie, abandon, reflection, and introspection in the rhythm of the heaving pulsebeat of nature is closely akin to that envisioned by Gustav Carus (1789–1869) as the proper province of the painter's efforts. According to Carus (*Nine Letters on Landscape Painting*, 1815–24), who was influenced by Friedrich, the "art of earth life" (*Erdlebenbildkunst*) should replace landscape painting, nature being subject to certain "transformations" (*Stadien des Naturlebens*)—development of species, decay, etc.—which can be connected with certain other natural changes—those of the atmosphere, the times of the day, etc. These "moods" are identical with human experiences (*Lebenszustände*) such as, for example, melancholy, apathy, elation. Runge's art, therefore, is not a completely isolated phenomenon but stands as a semireligious, scientific, aesthetic "experiencing of nature" at the beginning of the Romantic tradition of Steffens, Schelling, Friedrich, Carus, Heinrich, Dahl, Kersting. But Runge's "flower language" is quite unique, as are the abstract configurations of his later "landscape art." Also, while realistic, these two landscapes by Runge are "inventions," pure configurations of fantasy; Friedrich's landscapes may have, on occasion, some "added and invented" elements but are on the whole "views" of specific and existing nature attractions which he sought out and sketched on his many excursions into the country. Thus Friedrich's choice of subject matter was purely subjective.

Conversely, while his motivations originated in subjectivism, Runge strove for an objectively defensible and universally valid art. Runge used "views" principally only in his portraits. He neither painted any landscape compositions (as did Friedrich and his circle) in the conventional meaning of the word, nor did his theories call for such. Comparisons of Runge with such German landscapists as Koch, Hackert, Gessner, Reinhart, Rottmann, Preller, Schirmer, Goethe, Schütz, Klengel, Kobell, Oeser are therefore not called for. My view on this central and very controversial issue is corroborated by H. Schrade (*Die romantische Idee*, p. 44), G. Berefelt (*Bemerkungen zu Ph. O. Runge's Gestaltungstheorie*, p. 58, n. 46), G. Pauli (*Ph. O. Runges Zeichnungen*, pp. 17 ff.), and S. Waetzold (*Ph. O. Runges "Vier Zeiten,"* inaugural dissertation, Hamburg, 1951, pp. 17 ff.).

Runge follows up his own mystico-poetic speculation on *Die Quelle und der Dichter* with a long digression on Böhmian mythography. Whatever the precise interpretations of the two "Quelle" compositions themselves may be—and Runge is as "clear" on that issue as any of his biographers—they succeed in weaving a sensuously lyrical dream by which the spectator may easily be transported to follow the course of his own daydreams. Surely, Runge's intention to express "the idea of the first creation" must be comprehensive and broad enough to allow for the maximum of interpretational possibilities and for the optimum of extrapictorial associations; that implied abundance of ideational directions may be explored by each of us at leisure and in privacy.

Runge painted to *Die Quelle und der Dichter* a thematic pendant in *Die Ruhe auf der Flucht nach Ägypten* ("Rest on the Flight to Egypt"; 1805/06, oil on canvas, unfinished, 98 × 132 cm., Hamburg Kunsthalle, inv. no. 1004). The former was conceived by him as "Abend des Abendlandes" ("Evening of the Occident"), the latter as "Morgen des Morgenlandes" ("Morning of the Orient"). *Der Morgen* expresses in an abstract way the same ideational content found in *Ruhe auf der Flucht*, namely, the promise of the beginning of a new, universal life cycle.

The same great breadth and comprehensiveness of symbolic connotations can be claimed, with equal justification, of *Lehrstunde der Nachtigall* (*The Nightingale's Lesson*), which ranks as one of Runge's most completely finished paintings. (Second version; the first version burned in Munich in 1931; 1805, oil on canvas, 104.7 × 86.5 cm., Hamburg Kunsthalle, inv. no. 1009; cf. *H.S.*I, pp. 222 ff.) The picture was inspired by a poem by Klopstock which appears written on the inner tondo frame:

> "Flöten musst du, bald mit immer stärkerem Laute
> Bald mit leiserem, bis sich verlieren die Töne;
> Schmettern dann, dass es die Wipfel des Waldes durchrauscht—
> Flöten, flöten, bis sich bei den Rosenknospen verlieren die Töne.—"

> "You must flute, at times with strong sounds
> At times with softer ones, until the tones become lost;
> Then you must warble until the treetops resound—
> Flute, flute, until the tones vanish in the rosebuds.—"

The tondo is contained within a rectangular field in which are painted in monochromatic bas-relief imitation or the manner of a *trompe l'œil*, the coiling tendrils of lilies, roses, and oak leaves sprouting the figure of the "genie of the lily," a nightingale held on his finger, the "genie of the rose," and at the very top the figure of Amor playing the lute. The tondo itself contains, against a realistic background of dense foliage and a spring brook, the seated female figure of Psyche (or symbolically that of the Nightingale) giving instructions to Amor (or Cupid or symbolically "the little nightingale") perched on the branches above her and gazing intently into her eyes. Runge expresses here the thought of Psyche's instruction of Amor three times if the painting is read in consistency with his ideas of it, namely "that this picture will become exactly that which a fugue is in music." Pictorial composition and content structure based on the mechanics of musical composition, including variation, repetition, parallelism, and "counterpoint" movement are a strong influence on the artist and an important clue to the understanding of his iconography (*H.S.*I, p. 233). Following the pronouncement about the fugue, Runge says: "This has made me understand that the same thing happens in our art, namely how easy one can have it if one finds the musical sentence which underlies a whole composition and lets it appear again and again in variations throughout the whole composition." Runge's idea of motif repetition in effect parallels the leitmotiv techniques of a Weber, Berlioz, Wagner; he employs it in *Tageszeiten* (see below) most effectively.

Although both *Lehrstunde der Nachtigall* and *Die Mutter an der Quelle* as well as *Triumph des Amor* grew out of conventional mythographic symbolism, these pictures contain so much of Runge's own invention— new constellations of elements, the child and the child-flower composite symbols, undulating vegetal arabesques, amplification of iconographic meaning through "musical" techniques, the fusion of abstract design and two-dimensional space with naturalistic rendering and three-dimensional space—as to represent collectively a totally new departure in pictorial composition. As such they can be regarded as the beginning of a free or "open," that is, purely subjective, form of symbolism, one that, being a most significant new development of Romantic art, has diversified, enriched, and perpetuated modern art to our day. It must be added, however, that in that "open symbolism" already lie the seeds of the tragic dilemma of contemporary art—that which expands the expressive potential of the artist manyfold while simultaneously perplexing and alienating wider and wider segments of the population at large. Runge's "personal open symbolism" is the beginning of a long chain of artistic statements in recent history which have made the pathetic "misunderstood artist" the rule rather than the exception.

Runge summarizes his new beginning thus: "The whole thing would, for the time being, lead more to the arabesque and to hieroglyphics; however, out of it the landscape should develop, just as the historical composition developed from them. It is therefore not possible otherwise but that this art should be understood from the deepest mysticism of religion" (letter to Tieck, Dec. 1, 1802, *H.S.*I, p. 27). We have seen previously that Friedrich Schlegel, the most prolific art critic among the Romanticists of Runge's generation and the most outspoken defender of the Nazarene program with its attendant eclecticism, could not conceive of an art based on such a freely invented iconography and such ephemerally mystical premises (cf. Chapter III).

Runge was influenced by Tieck in the formulation of his ideas concerning "landscape." "I believe," he writes to him, "I am beginning to understand what you mean by landscape. In the whole course of history artists have always endeavored to see in human beings the movement of the elements of nature." But "the landscape would consist of the exact opposite, namely that people would see in all flowers and vegetation and in all natural phenomena only themselves and their passions" (ibid, p. 24). It is to be noted that Runge did not make the important distinction between landscape and nature. This fundamental attitude makes his problem, as our understanding of his solution, all the more difficult. No such difficulties are to be encountered when we read Tieck, Schlegel, Schelling, Novalis, or Brentano, for example, because the medium of language, unlike that of painting, fairly prevents such a confusion from ever arising in the first place. Nevertheless, Runge seems to have misunderstood Tieck after all.

We must therefore understand in the statement just quoted concerning landscape an overt implication regarding the "openness" of the new iconography which will be subject only to interpretations dictated by the personal inclinations and subjective leanings of the individual spectator, who, stimulated by the imagery before him, will lose himself with abandon in the daydreams, ideas, and psychic projections of his own making. The new iconography is in effect an instrument by means of which the spectator's imagination and creative impulses become unlocked to be free to roam the "landscape" of his own soul, an exercise, by the way, for which the restricted, fixed, and in literature rigidly circumscribed Graeco-Christian-Neoclassical iconography was rather ill suited. The subjection, therefore, of Runge's personal iconography to overenthusiastic attempts at scholarly codification, above and beyond that which Runge himself had to say on the subject, is an (all too common) error, one based on a misunderstanding of Runge's irrational premises. Conversely, we are all entitled and indeed encouraged by Runge to read whatever meaning into his pictures we might seriously care to consider, and particularly when he says: "Whatever spirit man puts [into the kingdoms of flora and fauna] that is the spirit they should have" (ibid, p. 24). Runge likens his allegorical creations to arabesques and hieroglyphs. Let us take him at his word and relate to the arabesques a sense of luxuriant abandon, of joyous surrender, of capitulation to the reasoned illogic of a design forever convoluted in labyrinthian perplexity and to the hieroglyphs a sense of mystery as behooves an honest-to-goodness emblematic riddle shrouded in enigma. It is true, of course, that Runge furnishes us with a running commentary on his creations, but this is only a beginning, an invitation to pursue the meanderings and peregrinations of our own poetic figments and religious phantasms.

In discussing Runge's *Tageszeiten*, Daniel comments that his brother allowed for interpretations and explanations of these drawings by others, because this is "in the spirit of the artist who liked to leave others the freedom to express the pure impressions which they have received from them" (*H.S.*I, p. 227). At another point Daniel writes: "The need for a closer interpretation and explanation of the details of the four pictures,

106

according to the nature of the allegorical, was felt deeply by all who saw them ever since their creation. Having felt this need, he thought of accompanying the four leaves at their publication with poetical commentary, which he planned to write in collaboration with Tieck, and perhaps even with musical compositions by Berger" (*H.S.*II, p. 471).

Runge's *Tageszeiten* ("Times of Day") cycle, his "magnum opus," consists of four drawings entitled *Morning, Evening, Noon,* and *Night.* It has perhaps received more attention from art historians than any other single German work of art. (*Der Morgen,* 1803, pen and ink, 72.1 × 48.2 cm., Hamburg Kunsthalle, inv. no. 34174; *Der Abend,* 1803, pen and ink, 72.1 × 48.2 cm., Hmbg. Kunsth., inv. no. 34170; *Der Mittag,* 1803, pen and ink, 71.7 × 48 cm., Hmbg. Kunsth., inv. no. 34177; *Die Nacht,* 1803, pen and ink, 71.5 × 48 cm., Hmbg. Kunsth., inv. no. 34181.) Runge painted two versions of *Der Morgen* ("Morning"): *Der Morgen* ("Kleine Fassung," with frame design), 1808, oil on canvas, 106 × 81 cm., Hmbg. Kunsth., inv. no. 1016; *Der Morgen* ("Grosse Fassung" without frame design), 1809, oil on canvas, unfinished, reconstitution of the dismembered painting from nine fragments, 115 × 111.5 cm., Hmbg. Kunsth., inv. no. 1022.

Isermeyer writes:

The *Four Times of Day* form the essential and determining center in Runge's work. His whole thought and activity was devoted to them as the purest manifestation of his inmost personality from the moment that he conceived them. They are the only work which he intended to be his confession before the public and as a contribution to art (*Philipp Otto Runge,* p. 43).

Compare this statement with the controversy about the place *Tageszeiten* should take up in "critical retrospective" of Runge's life, and, above all, to the views expressed on the topic by Böttcher (*Ph. O. Runge*). The four *Tageszeiten* drawings, along with the two painted versions of *Morning,* are the wish-come-true of the "creative iconologist," the sanction of any and all of his well-meant though all too often capricious thematic conjunctions in the name of iconographic exegesis, and a veritable fiat for the unlimited expansion of his scholarly profligacy for long times to come.

Let us begin our brief discussion of *Tageszeiten* by summarily stating that their symbolic content is sheerly inexhaustible (cf. especially *H.S.*I, pp. 31 ff.); Runge's poem on the *Tageszeiten, H.S.*I, pp. 52 ff.; also *H.S.*I, pp. 66 ff., 82 ff., 52 ff., 226–243; *H.S.*II, pp. 213 ff., 235 ff., 406, 468 ff.). Tieck says the following about *Tageszeiten:* "This vigorous Runge has produced in his *Tageszeiten,* which will soon appear as copper plates, something so original and new that it would be easier to write a book about these strange leaves, than to utter briefly something adequate about them" (*H.S.*II, p. 539). Goethe writes: "How much time and deep thought must not Runge have used on the *Tageszeiten*! They are a true labyrinth of darkling relationships, by their sheer unfathomability of meaning they seemingly cause vertigo, and yet the artist had in his work neither the prospect of profit nor any other cause except his pure love for the thing" (*H.S.*II, p. 529). Runge himself suggests that "So many remarkable compositions of things happen in them, which compositions again stand in an interconnection with each other, that I must never explain myself about it in detail; *these are merely the figures which are peculiar to my own nature*" (italics mine; letter to Daniel, June 1803, *H.S.*I, p. 47).

It seems that this statement is an additional corroboration of my thesis (cf. Chapter III, concluding paragraphs) that Runge's art must be considered as only *one* of many potentially possible specific applications of his general theory which allows for sheerly unlimited variations of "romantic" styles, symbols, subjects, and contents. But because Runge felt that the innermost spiritual contingencies of all people were identical at their core and because a language expressing those contingencies, if it flowed from the heart, had to reach the hearts of all people, he was also certain that those "figures peculiar to his nature" would not fail, sooner or later, to strike intelligible chords in kindred souls without extensive "rational objectivizations," which would fairly "lock up for him the living force of creation" (letter to Daniel, June 26, 1803, *H.S.*I, p. 48).

Man departs through the flat expression of his feelings or of his soul from the soul, and the glory of a time where such a poetry or such spirit exists is not far away. Exactly there is also the greatest darkness, because, while the world begins to understand it, the soul has already transgressed to the word and now gives birth to time from time, until the new birth of the soul. Therefore, I think, in symbolism or in poetry or the musical or mystical view of the three arts is to be found the preservation of the spirit of love, namely paradise (letter to Daniel, April 6, 1803, *H.S.*I, p. 44).

What Runge seems to be saying is in effect the following: we cannot now nor will we ever be able, by any means whatever, to determine the nature of man's "soul" in its mysterious primal ground; once that should occur man would cease to exist as man. And although Runge never determines explicit guidelines for a definitive iconographic exegesis of *Tageszeiten*, yet *Hinterlassene Schriften* provide enough leading projections as to induce their readers to drink from the Fountain of the Muses and to mount the Winged Pegasus for a soaring ride through Arcady.

But first it is mandatory, for a number of important reasons to be stated shortly, to give a detailed description of the four leaves; in addition, references will be made to Runge's usage of traditional iconography, and quotations will be cited from such of the artist's own exegeses as are specifically relevant to *Tageszeiten*.

In *Morning* a large ascending lily plant with four descending buds arising out of the light mist and clouds below represents the central motif. Four little children, playing the lute, double flute, triangle, and Panpipes, are seated on the arched bud tendrils, while the lily buds open up and scatter roses into the mist. Rising perpendicularly erect and on the central vertical axis stands the magnificent lily calyx (the traditional symbol of purity and virginity); upon its petals are seated six children in three groups, variably looking intently into each other's eyes, gazing into the depth of the calyx, or pointing upward to the filaments upon which stand three more child figures in intimate embrace holding up, at the apex of the composition, Venus or the Morning Star. A segment of the arching circumference line of the earth globe forming an infinitely expanding, abstract "landscape," and symmetrical masses of clouds rising upward from it, complete the elements of the inner picture. Both the lily and the segment of a circle as symbols of light and the earth, respectively, are derived from illustrations appearing in seventeenth-century Böhme editions. Runge gives us the following interpretation of it: "The light is the lily and the three groups, according to their disposition, again have a relationship to the Trinity. Venus is the pistil or the center of light and I have endeavored to give her no other form but that of the star. Just as the light here chases the color, so also does the color devour the light in the pendant, because that is the second [picture] or the Evening" (cf. letter to Daniel, Jan. 30, 1803, *H.S.*I, p. 31).

The frames of the four leaves are, according to Runge, instrumental in "indicating closer and larger relationships and transitions from one picture to the next" (cf. letter to Dr. Schildener, March 1806, *H.S.*I, p. 69). The frame of *Morning* contains at bottom center two crossed burning torches encircled by the ring of the serpent. (Traditionally, these are the symbols of Christ as the Light of the World and Satan.) The flames of the torch fade into the clouds on which, paired symmetrically on either side of the central vertical axis, a little boy and girl fly toward the corners on tiny Psyche wings. The rising borders are identical on both sides and consist of, reading from bottom to top, a lotus flower (which has no symbolic import in the Christian religion, but figures significantly in Buddhism and Hinduism as symbol of fertility; it is unlikely that Runge used the lotus in this or the Homeric sense as possessing the powers to induce forgetfulness), in which a seated child holds up, in the fashion of a standard, the stem and flower of the red amaryllis which bursts into blossom at the picture's midpoint. The amaryllis (traditional symbol of the Virgin) holds captive in the grasp of its stringlike pistils the figure of an upward looking child. Above this group arises the straight stem of the white lily, the calyx of which acts as a pedestal upon which a little angel, arms folded, kneels and bows in the uppermost corners of the frame compositions. Thus an angel appears bowing in each top corner, worshipping the centrally placed "supra porta" motif which consists of a shroud of angels' heads (traditional symbol of Paradise) surrounding a circular light bursting into a radiant aureole (traditional symbol of the persons of the Trinity) with the name JEHOVA inscribed within (cf. *H.S.*I, p. 227).

In the *Evening*, the upper central motif of *Morning*—the lily calyx with its nine child figures—appears at the bottom, sinking into the clouds and behind the partially visible, abstract symbol of the earth circle, which, as in the previous picture, implies an infinitely expanding, universal landscape. The star of Venus is now seen below the center of the composition as morning sinks into night. Also, the attitudes of the previously described child groups are changed. They now, respectively, embrace, sink into the calyx, and help lift the upper triad of children down from the pistils that support them. In the upper register of the picture all elements, particularly the vegetal ones, describe descending arcs, thus underscoring the "fall" of night. In *Morning*, conversely, all dominant lines accentuate a vertical or rising movement, thus lending impetus to the idea of the "rising" of day. On either side of the evening tableau symmetrically paired rose shrubs (the rose being the traditional symbol of martyrdom) sprout from the edges and decline in soft arcs toward the center, providing perches for six children who play the same instruments previously described, and trumpets. Above the roses appears the crowning motif, consisting of the widely arching leaves, tendrils, flowers, and buds of a poppy plant (the traditional symbol of sleep and the Passion of Christ) supporting two more children playing horns, two reclining children above them in the attitude of sleep, and the large majestic figure of a woman in the center. Behind and above her head appears the disc of the moon, while her outspread arms enfold a huge, dark, windblown shroud which is punctuated by tiny stars; thus the "mantle of evening," as it were, fills out the entire upper third of the composition.

Runge makes the following suggestions concerning symbolism: "As these two pictures [i.e., Morning and Night, to be taken up by us shortly] merely seek to pronounce the highest conception of the lily and the rose, and both only express the red color, so also follow two more pictures which express blue and yellow. The blue, in my opinion, dominates the day and the yellow the night" (cf. *H.S.*I, p. 32).

The frame of *Evening* contains in the center of the bottom border the Cross with the inscription INRI, the Crown of Thorns, and the eucharistic allusion of the Chalice. Little angels' heads with rosepetal wings appear on either arm of the Cross and roses sink into the Chalice. From this point on, moving toward the corners and in both side borders, all is again (as in all four pictures) symmetrically paired and nearly identical. A child seated in a mourning attitude upon the leaves of the aloe (symbol of sorrow; cf. p.

100) extinguishes a torch. The aloe raises its stem upward in the side border and drops, as if of blood, drip from its buds. In the center of the vertical risers appears a cluster of violets (traditional symbol of humility) upon which stands a child holding up, as if a banner, the stem and corolla of the larkspur (symbol of bravery; cf. p. 100). In the horizontal top border appears the figure of the Christchild (so identified by the Lamb, the symbol of the Christian banner) seated within a radiant aureole, while the uppermost corners each depict an angel in flight, looking downward, the opened calyx of a full-grown sunflower in his extended hands. (The sunflowers, in Runge's mind obviously symbols of the day, point downward just as they do in nature at the close of day; cf. *H.S.*I, p. 228.)

In *Noon* the lily appears once again but without child figures. It is encompassed by a large cornflower wreath which is seen as a perfect ellipse. The figure of a "mother" surrounded by a group of children, one of whom she breast-feeds, appears against the background of a hemispherical niche or arbor wrought of leaves and bordered by a horseshoe arch consisting of apricots, cherries, blueberries, plums, and grapes, obviously symbolizing the riches of the earth and harvest. Below the woman's feet a circular pool opens, fed by a water-spouting gargoyle-head at her feet. A profusion of nettles, violets, thistles (traditional symbols of sorrow, sin, and the Passion of Christ, respectively), bell-flowers, iris (symbol of purity), and hyacinths (symbol of prudence) completes the lower register of the composition. Above the arbor, the long reeds of the blue iris form an arch supporting at its crown two semireclining child figures who reach for the fruit offered them on an upturned flower calyx. Stalks of grain (allusion to the Eucharist here?) and flax complete the composition in the spandrel-like openings above the reed arch. Runge suggests that the picture is divided into a right male and a left female side, which is indicated by the sex of the children and the symbolic connotations of the flowers and herbs shown. Also, the species of the flowers and the attitudes of the children are to intimate "work and life," respectively (cf. *H.S.*I, pp. 35, 36).

In the frame of *Noon*, there appears at bottom center a flying angel, sword at the ready, defending the paradisiac rose aureole surrounding him. A kneeling child in each of the bottom corners busies himself tending a stalk of grain ears, from the midst of which the supple tendril of the mullein herb or velvet plant (its German name, *Königskerzenblume*, lends itself better to the symbolic portent of haughtiness or duplicity and infidelity) rises sinuously up the side border, a child trying in vain to climb to its bending crown. Above this motif, the vertical border contains some empty space and clouds, from which ascends the passion-flower, a snake coiling around its stem, its calyx supporting in both of the uppermost corners an angel worshipping the centrally placed triangle (traditional symbol of the Trinity) while kissing the roses sprouting therefrom. The triangle is surrounded by an aureole, before which is placed the semi-arc of the rainbow or the symbol of Peace (cf. *H.S.*I, p. 228).

Finally, in *Night* appears, in the bottom register, on either side, partly cut off by the inner frame, a foliage arbor below which a group of children sleep in hearty embrace. A third child, on either side, sleeps amid a profusion of lilies, sunflowers, cornflowers, firelilies, starflowers, auricles or primroses, thistles, storkbills, and thimbleweed. The central vertical axis consists of (from top to bottom) a sunflower, lilacs, night violets, and other flowers. Paired angels in descending arcs usher in the upper register which is composed of a large poppy plant, the center stalk of which is occupied by a large seated female figure representing night. On each of the plant's eight tendrils is seated a figure of a child, staring straight toward the spectator and gesturing variably with its hands. Over each of their heads appears a little star; the full moon is seen in the center (cf. *H.S.*I, p. 32). A. A. F. Milarch, a friend of Runge who wrote a long poetic-interpretive essay on *Tageszeiten* (*H.S.*II, pp. 530 ff.), had, according to Daniel (cf. *H.S.*II, p. 477), been told by the artist that the arcane meaning of these curious child figures was that of the "spirits of the stars, the judges of the life of the earth dwellers." In the frame we see at the bottom a fire fed by olive twigs (that tree being the traditional symbol of Divine Providence and Peace) the smoke of which billows toward the corners where, on each side, appears, perched on an olive tree branch, an owl. Disconnected from this bottom motif, appears, on either side in the risers, a vignette of flowers, including roses, cornflowers and marigolds (i.e. presumably red, blue and yellow; compare Chapter IV, p. 88) sprouting from an urn or vase (traditional symbol of fertility and the Annunciation) suspended in the air by little wings. Again disconnected from these, the top "supra porta" shows two groups of three child figures with Psyche wings (Faith, Love and Hope?) in worship of the Dove (or symbol of the Holy Spirit) which appears in the center and emits a radiant aureole of light beams (cf. *H.S.*I, p. 229).

We have provided the reader with the detailed description of the four leaves for the following reasons: (1) The customary one: conventional iconological methodology requires the full identification of all elements prior to their symbolic interpretation. (2) To form a solid basis upon which Runge's symbolic interpretations and those of others may be compared and critically judged. (3) To prevent a common pitfall: Runge scholars, relying on the hopeful but erroneous assumption that their readers will identify all objects for and by themselves (in the small, often "illegible" reproductions available to them in books) seldom trouble themselves to provide such descriptions, but rather start off at the "deepest end" with inscrutably rendered, darkling propositions concerning symbolism, thus losing the understanding of even the most sympathetic reader from the start. (4) To provide the reader, who may not be all too familiar with flower and herb species, with their appropriate names so that he may decide for himself whether or not Runge's hieroglyphics composed of the flower and the flower-figure composite symbols indeed represent a viable language that can readily be adopted for communication.

Hubert Schrade voices the following sober note concerning *Tageszeiten*:

If we realize Runge's viewpoint in its totality, as well as the seriousness with which he invested the practise and the observation of art, we will be extremely surprised by those leaves. They are arabesques, full of mystery but also full of *playfulness*, they are too *ornamental* in order to act as a vision, too *abstract* and *compounded* in order to really represent the suggested realities (italics mine; *Die Romantische Idee von der Landschaft*, p. 55).

"Playful," "ornamental," "abstract," "compounded," exactly that way did the large folio leaves appear to me when I viewed them in the Hamburg Kunsthalle. I can easily sympathize with anyone free from prejudices based on a reading of *Hinterlassene Schriften*, who sees in the *Tageszeiten* pleasant designs for bookcover, plaque, door or wall decorations, and not much more than that. Conversely, the paintings of *Der Morgen*, particularly the large version, will impress anyone extremely by the sheer purity of their colors and uniqueness of lighting.

The question whether Runge's personal symbols consisting of flowers and child figures represent a viable artistic language in the service of the artist's own purposes, can easily be verified by the reader by simply comparing his own impressions received so far with Runge's definition of *Tageszeiten* to "check out" possible interpretational discrepancies: "*Morning* is the unbounded illumination of the universe. *Day* is the unbounded forming of the creature which fills the universe. *Evening* is the unbounded destruction of existence into the origin of the universe. *Night* is the unbounded depth of the knowledge of the unextirpated existence of God. These are the four dimensions of the created spirit. But God works all in all; who can form as He touches the formed?" ("Rubrics to the Times of the Day," *H.S.*I, p. 82).

This writer, for one, would not receive, judging from the pictures alone, the same impression, if his familiarity with Runge's mystical ideas did not in some measure conduce to point him, more or less, in that general or similar direction. Of course, the average viewer lacks that insight, would therefore stray much farther from Runge's intended meaning. It is true that any good compendium of religious signs and symbols will provide much information about traditional flower symbolism and its varieties assigned to given botanical species in religious art (e.g., George Ferguson, *Signs and Symbols in Christian Art*; Hans Aurenhammer, *Lexikon der Christlichen Ikonographie*; Karl Künstle, *Ikonographie der Christlichen Kunst*).

However, Runge uses his flowers in this, at least in principle, "internationally codified" manner only in small part, the rest being based on national, regional, and colloquial flower names and their folklore meanings. We cannot even be sure exactly when and at what instance Runge uses his flowers in the first (traditional) or the second (free or open) sense in any of the four compositions. This adds to the confusion. Therefore, the associative meanings a given spectator may ascribe to Runge's flowers will vary according to his personal "reading" of the traditional and free symbolic meanings in a manner indigenous to his native region and according to how his fancy strikes him. It can therefore be concluded that Runge's flower language is deficient in its ability to communicate directly, connotatively, and universally and that his *idée fixe* of expressing a host of definite primary and associative meanings in rebuslike hieroglyphic flower puzzles proves to be a practical failure.

This does not mean, however, that a familiarity with Runge's flower interpretations (as far as such a one can be obtained from *Hinterlassene Schriften* at all), an insight into the conventional language of symbolic signs and artifacts, and a knowledge of Runge's own mystagogical thought constructs relating to the Bible, Böhmian phantasmagoria, and the mysticism of color and geometric figures may not incite those of a speculative turn of mind and with a penchant for polemical conjecture worthy of the undertaking to strike out on their own and indulge in further thought on the subject. It seems that Runge began a trend characterizing so much of modern art, particularly in the twentieth century, which requires the services of the artist as "interpreter" of his art, which provides printed "programs" for gallery visitors, and which makes—in what seems to be a democratic situation though one which lacks standards, maxims, and criteria of objective evaluation—art critics of all people in their own and just rights. The following is an attempt at summarizing my own impressions about the symbolic content of *Tageszeiten*, as well as the most important of those theories which have been advanced to this date.

Among the potentially best of such "speculative minds" who would have cherished the idea of interpreting Runge's work, would undoubtedly have been that of Schopenhauer. Compare in this regard his enthusiastic endorsement of a romantically ambiguous art of allegorizing hieroglyphs (*Sinnbilder*) in opposition to Winckelmann's views of a classically unequivocal art (Schopenhauer, "Die Welt als Wille und Vorstellung," *Sämtliche Werke*, pp. 314 ff.). My discussion of the *Tageszeiten* symbolism is principally based on the following sources: Daniel's "Lebensgänge des Verfassers," *H.S.*II, pp. 468 ff.; "Aus dem Programm zur Jenaischen Allgemeinen Literaturzeitung von 1807: Unterhaltung über Gegenstände der bildenden Kunst," *H.S.*II, pp. 514 ff. (this last mentioned source is signed W.K.F., i.e., *Weimarer Kunstfreunde*, and therefore represents

Goethe's "official opinion"); "Aus den Heidelbergischen Jahrbüchern der Literatur von 1808: Philologie, Historie, Literatur und Kunst, Erster Jahrgang, Zweites Heft" by J. Görres, *H.S.*II, pp. 515 ff.; J. M. Speckter's article in *Nieder-Elbische Merkur* (p. 96); compare *H.S.*II, pp. 526 ff. Milarch's, Tieck's, and Chateauneuf's interpretations (cf. *H.S.*II, pp. 530 ff., 538 ff., 540 ff.). In addition I have used the following recent contributions to the special problem of Runge's personal iconography: J. Langner, *Philipp Otto Runge in der Hamburg Kunsthalle*, Bilderhefte der Hamburger Kunsthalle IV; S. Waetzold, *Ph. O. Runges "Vier Zeiten"*; A. Aubert, *Runge und die Romantik*; W. Roch, *Philipp Otto Runges Kunstanschauung*; C. Grützmacher, *Novalis und Philipp Otto Runge*; H. Börensen, *Der Morgen von Philipp Otto Runge*; G. Berefelt, *Bemerkungen zu Ph. O. Runges Gestaltungstheorie*; K. K. Eberlein, *Runges Tageszeiten. Das Gesamtkunstwerk der Romantik* (in *Der Wagen*, 1933).

Runge attempted to express in his *Tageszeiten* in a symbolic or allegorical way the infinite life of nature as it relates to her revelation, eternal redemption, and sanctification of the world on the basis of those elements provided by her and known to all. He subjected the form of the work to a strict geometric symmetry and architectonic regularity for purposes of clarity, and in order thus to prevent the possibility of endless "visual rumination." "I believe firmly that the strict regularity is needed most of all in works of art which flow from the imagination and the mystique of our soul without external subject matter [*äusseren Stoff*] or history" (letter to Daniel, Dresden, Feb. 13, 1803, *H.S.*I, p. 35). For an interpretive discussion of the geometric construction of *Tageszeiten*, compare Stephan Waetzold, *Philipp Otto Runges "Vier Zeiten" und ihre Konstruktionszeichnungen* (pp. 234–247). In his discussion of Runge's style in *Tageszeiten*, Pauli (*Ph. O. Runges Zeichnungen*) thinks that the artist's meticulous structural measurements (of which numerous, highly complex ones have survived) "cool off our feelings" considerably. Pauli further comments that Runge was unable to bring into a satisfactory union the classic academic heritage with his own genius for the flowing, Gothic form, and therefore his decorative works appear torn between the two; they appear as a mixture of the "Italian grotesque" and "late-Gothic–Dürer-like vegetal ornament."

The rhythm and harmony of the cycle of drawings is based on Runge's musical, eurhythmic or "fugal" compositional theories, and on the organic-architectonic contingencies to which natural vegetal life is subject in an intrinsic fashion owing to the mechanics of botanical growth patterns (cf. supra; cf. Chapter III). "Runge's *Four Times of Day* leaves are merely the score. A score which one must be able to read, not only as a sign language of his ideas and thoughts, but also as a notation of his tones and colors" (K. K. Eberlein, *Runges Tageszeiten*, p. 21).

Runge writes:

I beg you not to see only the most noteworthy [vegetal forms] but also, if you only possibly can, to seek and note the architectonic stability and configuration of the plant. The naïveté of composition is often admirable and I, for my part, believe that in order for it to move charmingly in decorative works it is very necessary to have insight into botanical forms; while a representation may be composed of ever so many objects, yet, the true total form still is a vegetal plant (letter to Klinkowström, June 13, 1808, *H.S.*I, p. 176).

It may be added that Runge, ever since his childhood and on to his last days in life, studied, silhouetted, drew, and constructed all botanical specimens available to him and, if they were not, requested others to provide him with samples or detailed reports of them, so that he might draw them himself.

The religious meaning of the whole cycle must be related to the peculiarities of Christian symbolism in general, as well as to Runge's personal religious allegories in particular. The symbolism arising out of Runge's insistence on a parallelism existing between the "colors of the day," the basic "colors of the palette," and the "colors of flowers" should be interpreted according to, and understood in keeping with, Runge's arcane undulations of purpose and intent. If all this is taken into account, then the expanded meaning of *Tageszeiten* corresponds to the seasons or the periods of bloom, production, bearing, and destruction (cf. *H.S.*II, pp. 476 ff.). Moreover, an analogy between the above and the periods of man's life—childhood, youth, manhood and old age—has been proposed. In this connection *Morning* can be likened to the coming of light and perception, *Noon* to comprehension, *Evening* to reflection, and *Night* to knowledge. Beyond that, analogies to the life and Passion cycles of Christ, to His enigmatic utterings concerning the flow of world history as a change of cosmic seasons, have been suggested. In turn, biblical exegesis, along with Romantic predilections for a vitalist concept of history as that of an organic-dynamic-cyclical process, has also given rise to the reading of *Tageszeiten* as an entelechy immanent in "world seasons," that is, as creation, growth, decline, and fall of entire peoples and civilizations. If this still does not satisfy the most speculative minds among us, the cycle may express, in addition, time and eternity and the basic idea of the original connection between man and God in the youth of humanity (and in that of the individual), his separation from God at midpoint of the world-historical day and in life, and his return to God in the "evening." I have indicated in my first chapter that in order to do justice to our topic it is necessary to have, among other attributes, passionate objectivity and a sense of humor. Now is the time to employ these faculties.

Daniel Runge summarizes these analogies as follows: (1) "The birth, premonition and perception of the light in the morning of life, youth and innocence." (2) "The futile efforts during the day of life to arrive through one's own efforts alone at the concept and knowledge of the highest good" which causes the "errors, separation and rupture as well as human suffering." (3) "The grace and compassion of the Saviour" which comes "in the evening of life." And finally (4) "the consoler, the Holy Spirit, in time and eternity" from which again grows the new dawn (ibid., p. 476). We cannot deny that Daniel's sentiments, in and by themselves as a philosophical insight of an ontological nature, have much to recommend them as an attractive *Weltanschauung*. But can we in all seriousness establish a connection between them and the drawings? I cannot. Daniel recapitulates his emanative ideas as follows: the first two drawings express God's creation and preservation, the third conciliation and redemption, the fourth perfection and sanctification. In addition, Runge was to have expressed this process through the symbolism of color, its five elements, and all its nuances.

In order to summarize the most recent state of the problem to its simplest form, and to reduce the endlessly meandering propositions advanced by talented scholars, the following "equation" may be helpful:

Morning = spring = birth and childhood = creation = becoming;
Noon = summer = active life = Old Testament = life;
Evening = fall = *Liebestod* ("love death") = New Testament = perfection;
Night = winter = death = eternal life = chaos.

We might, of course, wonder, if this is indeed the way in which we should understand the *Tageszeiten* cycle, why Runge did not provide us with a coherent outline for its correct interpretation and thus prevent excessive speculation. His answer: "If I had wanted to say it, it would not be necessary for me to paint it" (*H.S.*II, p. 472). This is an observation which Daniel follows up by saying: "Which does not, however, exclude the fact that he would have liked to have seen and would have received it in a friendly manner if others also expressed in words the results of their own meditative observations of his pictures, as long as this was done in a healthy spirit and according to each individual's personal manner of perception and expression." Runge's wish has been fulfilled.

Stephan Waetzold (*Philipp Otto Runges "Vier Zeiten,"* p. 1) takes the just quoted statement by Runge as the raison d'être for his dissertation. He argues that, unlike most writers, he would not approach Runge's art from his theories but "the other way around," and he adds: "It would be wrong, if as is done again and again in literature, we base our judgment of Runge's work solely on his art theories." It is also precisely my thesis that Runge's work should be discussed separately from and independently of his theories. But Waetzold, nevertheless, falls into the same trap of over-interpretation and overestimation of Runge's work into which, as he correctly observes, have fallen his predecessors. His crafty argument, namely, if it is carried out in its consequences, could never result in a lengthy dissertation, but least of all in one that bristles with quotations from *Hinterlassene Schriften* and from nearly all the Runge literature. A dissertation based on the Waetzold premise, which I heartily support, could probably not exceed a few dozen pages; anything beyond that would be fiction. It is due to Waetzold's talent for establishing thematic analogies, contextual parallelisms, and interpretational conjunctions, and to his fine style, that his work, despite its inherent illogic, is nevertheless very enjoyable and rewarding reading as one of the most exhaustive iconographical studies of Runge's *Tageszeiten* to this day.

In "Die Deutungen der Radierungen als Zyklus" (pp. 108 ff.) Waetzold offers his major proposition according to which the *Tageszeiten* cycle should be interpreted. This is his *Polaritätsgedanke* ("idea of polarities"), a notion (one based, incidentally, on Runge's own nomenclature which is characterized by an excessive concentration of semantically opposing extremes) which consists of the evaluation of "opposites," that is, of natural and abstract elements, contour and plasticity, surface and space, and thematic contrasts. Concerning the contents of *Tageszeiten*, Waetzold summarizes (p. 181): "That content is given to us in the concept of polarity, that of vital powers of love and light, in the cosmic rhythm of becoming, being and passing away, and eternal duration, in the motion of rise and fall, in stability and radiant emission and finally in the light-color and the symbolic figures of the paintings." It may be added that this striking phraseology is uncomfortably close to that of Runge's own, in fact, so much so, that it is difficult to accept it as the result of Waetzold's premise.

It was Runge's plan, almost from the time of his initial conception of *Tageszeiten* as drawings, to translate the project into paintings. He proposed the general tones of the four paintings to be of the colors of (1) the "misty-reddish dawn," (2) the "sunshine with clear skies," (3) the "reddish dusk meeting the moon," and (4) the "burning fire, smoke and dew."

The first picture (*Morning*) I ask you to consider as approximately a view such as is caused by the sun, which rises above the morning fog; to think of it in such a manner that the spheric section of the earth rolls like a distant mountain in the mist of the dawn; the foreground formation would be merely an arabesque alluding to the background. The second (*Day* or *Noon*) would be seen in pure sunshine and clear skies, a day when the pollen permeates the air," etc. "The third (*Evening*) would appear in its colors in such a manner as if the evening glow had equal brilliance with the glow of the moon in the sky and the shine of both would fuse; the colors of the flowers and the tones of the instruments would imitate this mood.

118

The fourth (*Night*) would at the bottom light up in a fire, a fire of flowers which would concentrate where the sleeping figures are; they may be certain of love and protection which comes from above us quietly and eternally and in which, always anew and in a perpetual circle, all will blossom, beget and again perish (letter to Schildener, March 1806, *H.S.*I, pp. 68 ff.).

It has been indicated previously that the perfection of his ambitious color theory was the most important prerequisite for the execution of this undertaking. Therefore the completion of the paintings was much delayed and we are very fortunate to have two, partially completed paintings, namely the two versions of *Morning*, known as the *Little Morning* (with frame) and the *Large Morning* (without frame). (Cf. inventory descriptions, p. 107.) It is significant to note that by divesting the second version of the cumbersome symbolical frame apparatus, Runge not only simplified the purely artistic resolution of the whole problem, but also, as has been pointed out already, it indicates that he moved steadily away from the excessively mystical and intractable in his later years.

The additional difficulties arising out of the rendering in color, perspective, value, and volume of both the *Morning* drawing and its frame (for both are rendered naturalistically) along with the aforementioned symbolic apparatus caused great strains on Runge's ability to maintain a stylistic cohesion of the whole work. The problem that confronted him can easily be regarded as one of the most if not the most difficult of problems ever undertaken in art. Both the large and small version of *Morning*, with the exception of the frame, are very similar to each other and vary only in relatively small details if we disregard the difference in the dimensions. The frame of the *Small Morning* differs from the frame of the drawing in that it is changed in detail and considerably simplified. The crossed burning torches at the bottom of the drawing are replaced by a magnificent sun in eclipse. Two child genies flee from the dark disc with its radiant corona toward the sides where, in each corner, a child sits entrapped in the roots of the lotus flower. The upper register of the frame is identical with the drawing in all objects depicted, although their forms differ somewhat.

The two paintings differ dramatically from the drawing. The panoramic spectacle of a *real*, illusionistic, infinite landscape, a vista created through atmospheric and linear perspective opens before our eyes, a spectacle which stands in total contrast to the two-dimensional, linear, abstract contour rendering of space and objects in the drawing. It is as if suddenly the sun had burst from the clouds, as if a mighty musical chorale had shattered the silence, as if a thousand voices at once were animating the stillness which had prevailed; all breathes and pulsates with life. Through the beauty of his pure colors and a formal simplicity, Runge enhanced here the visual immediacy and dramatic impact (both lacking almost totally in

the drawing) to a degree that has not failed to startle, delight, and lasting-
ly impress all those who have seen the paintings. The newborn child, lying
on its back upon the verdant foliage, appears in the foreground and sym-
bolizes the awakening morning of life; symmetrically paired children offer
roses to the baby. Venus or the Morning Star has assumed corporeality in
the large, sensuously beautiful female figure appearing in the center of the
painting. Above her, suspended in the air, appears a large lily calyx with
children seated upon its petals. But now the lily acts as that brilliant source
of light that Runge intended it to be from the time of his original conception
of the work. The triad of children above this motif appears in free flight
and in the motion of a joyous dance; the children gaze upward toward a
tiny golden star. Strangely, it seems, that Runge now reverts to expressing
with human forms that which he set out to visualize only with flowers.
For the sunrise is embodied by the figure of Venus (who is also Urania,
Mother Earth, Aurora); but Aurora the bringer of the morning light is
also the Virgin Mary, the harbinger of the Light of the World, and the
real child at her feet is the embodiment of the Christchild, the hope of a
new dawn (cf. *H.S.*I, p. 229).

These two paintings are completely different in their effect on the
spectator from anything I have seen in nineteenth-century art. They differ
particularly from anything French art has produced during that period.
The subtlety of hue variations, the delicacy of value blending, the fineness
of chromatic scaling, the great complexity of light and shadow constellations, the plasticity of figures and the spaciousness of the infinite landscape, the completely unusual and extraordinary subject matter, the over-
all feeling of "transcendence" in a union of the real and the ideal—all these
are so startling in their effect as to mark these two last works by Runge as
standing in a class of painting all their own. I cannot think of any work
with which to compare them.

Runge's artistic oeuvre remained a fragment; he did not finish the
ambitious task which he set for himself, for perhaps it can never be finished.
And that may be its most remarkable characteristic. It merely represents a
wish, a longing, a romantic dream: one man's soaring, if brief, flight into
the sunrise of a new morning on the Icarus wings of romantic inspiration.

CONCLUSION

*A*S with any critical discussion involving the qualitative analysis of an artist, movement, style, genre, or form of art, so also in our case, the scope as well as the limitations of attainable results should be recognized and established in advance of the investigation. The feeling of ennui often expressed by those emerging from a colloquium, or the experience of reading polemical essays in the history of art, is based largely on an oversight of that requirement and besides on a fundamental misunderstanding that results from false premises germane to the topic of art as such. As a consequence weariness manifests itself—and a yearning for concrete effects with an objectively determinable bearing on material reality. But even as art itself merely has an inner purpose distinguished by autonomous consequences and exclusive congruities which constitute no verifiable antecedents to an exactly definable outward utility, just so must we understand our discussions involving art. Thus, it is incompatible with the nature of the objects being considered, much less with their underlying theories, to arrogate to such discussions a role that transcends those objects' manifest essence, one which has no measurable practical bearing on reality.

At best and under conditions of good will all around, such investigations may lead to certain purely personal results based on the individual needs and efforts of the participant in the dialogue and affecting his subjective posture according to the peculiar nature of his subconscious inclinations but never by fiat of verifiable or universally binding laws. These laws thought to be necessary postulates by many nineteenth-century Romantic idealists as moral support for their occasional creative desultoriness, have been uncovered as a superfluous adjunct to total artistic freedom and the libertine experience of its products in the twentieth century. Because of the present state of absolute aesthetic relativity and because, moreover, a discussion of art theory stands to objective reality in a relationship that is possibly twice further removed from it than art itself, it is both inappropriate and futile, even under the most propitious circumstances, to seek on pragmatic grounds for a specific utility in interpretive disputations on art. Thus whatever satisfaction or utility one might be able to extract from such exercises does not rest on the outer logic of the work of art and consequently not on that of deliberations about it—the existence of neither one or the other can be demonstrated—but rather must be posited on the inner logic and private purposiveness of productive individual perception. Exponents of a critical history of art should, it seems, stress above all that aspect of creativity both with regard to their own method of investigation as well as to the way they would prefer to be approached by others.

I would like to introduce my concluding summary with a retrospective thought about my methodology of analysis. It is first of all necessary to arrive at the proper framework and appropriate procedural method before a meaningful discussion of Runge's contribution to the theory of art can even begin to take place. This may sound like a truism of questionable merit in a formal discourse, but in the special case of Runge and in view of the literature concerned with him, it is not as undoubted and self-evident a fact as might appear on the surface. On the contrary. All too often the obvious is not being applied by scholars as the yardstick of measurement because of an understandable but unfortunate confusion of disparate categorical relevancies. Because Runge's collective oeuvre is characterized by an innate bifurcation into theory and practice, writing about, and creation of art, I have followed what seems to me the appropriate methodology germane to him. Accordingly, I have above all stressed this basic division and distinguished sharply between the critique of Runge's theories, on the one hand, and of his work, on the other. No undue and unwarranted overlapping of these two categories needs to or should occur. In that manner alone can Runge's theoretical writings be appraised for their indigenous value without the unnecessary distractions and irrelevant considerations tending to obscure so much of the scholarly discussion of Runge's theories. Only in that manner can Runge's theoretical contributions be judged solely on their intrinsic merit without the prevalent yet needless obfuscation.

That this procedure, which commends itself for its logic on general principle alone, has not been used specifically in the evaluation of Runge's theories so far, is no doubt largely due to the fact that it is very difficult to apply unremittingly to Runge's seemingly inchoate *Hinterlassene Schriften*. And here I hope to have demonstrated that such results as are commensurate with our objectives and methodology can best be achieved if in our critical reading of *Hinterlassene Schriften* we separate judiciously all that which appears to be of general import, timeless value, and universal applicability, from that which is only limited and dated in its importance for us today. Into the latter category I have grouped major portions of the excessively mystical, exotic, abstruse, recondite, and capricious passages, including large sections of Runge's ruminating discussions of his personal iconography. While a certain danger of subjectivism and bias which this critical method harbors cannot be denied, especially when it is applied unscrupulously, it appears that the advantages of such "interpretive editing" sympathetic to Runge are ever so much greater, in defining and bringing us closer to an understanding of the cogent parts of Runge's theories, as to outweigh these minor and avoidable pitfalls.

Following in the order of importance the concerns of methodology and the selective approach to a critical reading, I have taken prefatory issue, as it bears weight on Runge, with one of the most unwieldy problems besetting art historians, namely, the categorization of the "three great isms" of nineteenth-century art. In doing that I have shown that the pluralistic conflux of Romanticism, Classicism, and Realism in the collectively so-called Romantic art of Germany, being far from exceptional, rather represents its very operating principle. Therefore, rather than being antagonistic and antipodal in relation to each other, these three "isms" are entwined in intimate contiguity. If this was shown to be consistent with evidence on general grounds, it was doubly true for Runge. We have seen that Runge combines in his theories all three elements with all their attending qualifications and that that unified, concordant, or total aesthetic approach is the most distinguishing characteristic of his theory. Thus it can be concluded that an atomist art historical doctrine will fail to unravel the meaning of German Romanticism as it will miss fathoming Runge's theories in their intended purpose.

If, in conclusion, the above premises are taken once more as valid departures, then we can proceed in recapitulating and emphasizing what appear to be the most salient features of Runge's contributions as theorist, and we can evaluate his importance for our time.

The nineteenth century witnessed the decline and fall of hoary traditions in virtually all fields which vitally affect man's corporate and private lives: feudalism yielded to parliamentary government, Christianity succumbed to Enlightenment ethics, philosophical determinism acquiesced in the pursuit of freedom, man's natural environment submitted to the ravages of the Industrial Revolution. In the wake of uncertainty, restiveness, anxiety, and hopeful anticipation, the age saw the last vestiges of medieval political and societal patterns wither, theological postulates collapse, cultural norms alter; indeed, the very ecological balance was violated. The times called for a nearly total re-examination of man's relationship to himself, to his fellow man, to God, and to nature. It was incumbent upon the artist to translate into visual imagery the radical ideational departures of his epoch. And Runge, foreseeing much of what the future held in store, engaged deeply in this dialogue of reappraisal. Keenly sensing the need for a radically different art serving the needs of the dawning New Age, he formulated the most challenging revolutionary proposals for the institution of a new theoretical basis for art, one that would reflect and express the changed condition of man in his universe.

Runge broke violently with tradition. Being oriented solely toward the future in his thinking, he held out no hope for the restoration of the traditional art form or for the rehabilitation of the conventional iconographic apparatus. Convinced that neither could function meaningfully in his time, Runge rejected all thought of eclecticism and retrogressive historicism. He had no predecessors in art whom he could have used as models, points of reference, or agents of corroboration for his uniquely individualistic theories.

Although it would be wrong, of course, because of his education, reading, and admiration of a few artists of the High and Late Renaissance, to attribute to him a state of *tabula rasa*, we have seen that he was a "primitive" of a special kind, nevertheless. Runge was indebted to certain of his contemporaries for spiritual and philosophical stimulation, as we have shown in considerable detail. However, he had to invent and formulate all of his ideas and concepts himself for their specific application to and use in art which, being concerned with, among other things, the symbolic concretion and visual manifestation of ideational constructs, requires the re-translation of the verbalized idea to optical apprehension. That this is especially true of the highly literary, meditative, and speculative Romantic art in Germany, of which Runge represents the most notable example, has been adequately demonstrated in my discussion. Runge was concerned in this regard with the maximum subjective individualism of artistic expression and with the optimum objective universalism of spectator comprehension. Thus he was as truly original as he was farsighted, by taking issue with the cardinal dilemma of contemporary art in its predicament of spectator reaction to completely free artistic expression.

Runge built his aesthetics on the foundations of Christianity. But because Christianity for him was neither a subject for academic disputation by philosophers nor a matter of sanctimonious lip service, but rather a way of life, an absolute mandate for the physical, moral, ethical, civic, and aesthetic conduct and development of man, a sacred covenant with God, he was above all anxious to bring art into agreement with his ideology and thereby to achieve the only genuine art possible for him. An art not springing from the roots of personal ideology would be a lie according to him. But because his ideology *was* Christianity, regardless of the specific peculiarities with which he invested that faith and notwithstanding all other religions, Runge anticipated a contemporary trend in art which recognizes the complete legitimacy and credibility of a work of art only on condition of its full accordance and identity with the *Weltanschauung* of the artist, whatever its special properties. Runge not only articulated this doctrine of spiritual authenticity often but also made it the keystone of his theory.

The factors and qualities which attend Runge's mystically intuited religious convictions, particularly with respect to their outward effects in human conduct and relations, are astonishing in their modern sound. In this regard it would be well to emphasize that Runge's ethics and his aesthetics were predicated on identical feelings and that his so-conceived supra-idealistic inspiration for art had to emanate from the moral impulse. Thus Runge's ideas about the immediate consequences of the Christian position should have a special interest for us in the great weight they bear on his art theories. In attempting to bridge the gulf which separates the real from the ideal, the absolute from the relative, active engagement from detached contemplation—a schism which was intensified with the confrontation of post-Kantian absolute idealism (of which Runge had a general conception if not detailed knowledge) and the demands of an activist "practical Christianity" as a way of life (which Runge firmly believed and diligently followed in his own life)—in attempting to neutralize those polarities then, Runge points the way toward the resolution of the Existentialist dilemma: wary of excessive abstractions and "philosophizing," Runge urges the artist to seek the concrete experience. *Hinterlassene Schriften*, which are punctuated by his counsel for sincerity in conduct, genuine expression of feeling, active involvement and participation in the real, meaningful, selfless, intensive, and authentic situation with fellow man and God, anticipate modern Christian Existentialism. Runge understood love as the unconditional surrender of one's own identity to the other, precisely therefore not a subject-object but rather the Existentialist "I-Thou," subject-subject relationship. He saw in the mystery of that enigmatic state also the modus operandi of the aesthetic function. A subjective artistic language so based on the inmost feelings would, according to Runge, enable man to communicate with his fellow man in a truly authentic manner and therefore with objectively determinable, universal validity. In this way Runge opens the road toward personal expression in art, toward artistic self-expression free from the fetters of officially or academically prescribed aesthetic criteria, regardless of the prevalent "ism" they may advocate. In freeing art from parochialism and affected allegiances to doctrinaire partisanships, Runge subjected it to the severe scrutiny of the individual artist's conscience. Realizing the great responsibility this placed on the artist, Runge was doubly eager for him to command over such spiritual resources as would enable him to bear that weight; but because art is almost as important for Runge as life itself, it follows that no less than the unreserved commitment of a fully comprehensive world ideology could guarantee that hypostatic reserve. And that for Runge was Christianity.

Runge championed an art as tool for the release of, and means of sustenance for, psychic impulses commanded by the immediate exigencies in the life of the artist and present at the moment of creation. It was therefore axiomatic for him also to advocate a free or (what I have termed) open symbolism, as opposed to the restrictive, stringently circumscribed traditional symbolism. Runge anticipated in this counsel Post-Impressionist developments. Such an open symbolism, according to Runge, provided it was founded on genuinely sincere feelings and an honest desire to communicate, would enrich and vastly expand the entire scope of art. In accurately prophesying the death of traditional anthropomorphic art and its panoply of figurative symbolic representations, Runge ushered in the new, non-homocentric or Christian landscape art, as he called it. This art would no longer avail itself of the conventional and systematized iconographic apparatus, but rather would formulate a new animistic symbolism, one based on nature's own and universally known elements and standing in close analogy to the artist's personal, deeply felt, intuited wonder about God's creation. Such a symbolism would enable him to form nature into art much more comprehensively than was ever possible for him to do with the traditional signs and symbolic personifications.

Runge's theories on landscape art can indeed summarily be regarded as expressing "nothing less than the modern feeling" for nature, a nature not regarded as man's static, inanimate, spatial extension and thus subject to his constant modifications, but rather as a dynamic, living, mysterious, challenging, revealing panorama, an autonomous organism splendid in its grandeur yet synergistically coupled with and reflecting man's deepest drives. Whether Runge succeeded with his symbolical compositions in conveying such a meaning of an objective-universal-typical landscape, or whether they are merely the products of a purely subjective-personal-specific expression is a central issue in Runge scholarship. Whatever the final verdict on Runge's practical efforts in that direction may be (and limiting qualifications have been raised by me regarding his ultimate success), we have demonstrated that the theories upon which these efforts were based laid down as their final goal a new landscape art consisting entirely of fully abstract elements of form, conveying a new romantic-vitalist-ontological-cosmological concept of nature to be understood in its meaning through immediate apprehension and spontaneous cognition.

In close correspondence to the issues of the new symbolism and the new landscape stand Runge's propositions regarding their implementation into the reality of a new artistic language. And here we have found that Runge unequivocally stated many original and modern thoughts. Above all, in this connection, I must cite his natural inclination for and concept of synesthesia. Through the simultaneous experiencing of phenomena by means of all sensory faculties the artist could experience nature more fully and deeply. By using such appropriate symbols as connote their various sensory origins, the artist could stimulate kindred responses of the spectator's sensory organs. But the critically delicate point of transition from perception to material form lies, according to Runge, beyond all rationalization in the zone of creative inspiration. Runge's desire to encompass the whole broad spectrum of human sensations into a unified and intensified experience resulted in his synesthesia. In close relationship to it, and to his insistence upon the optimal possible subjective sensory, intellectual, and emotional receptiveness, stands his equally inclusive need for the study of the objective world in the maximum number of its possible aspects and revelations in nature. Finding the nominalist-atomist notions about the nature of phenomena as mere compound aggregates of separately determinable particles, psychologically unfounded stereotypes, he relied on his mystical intuition which sought for the wider configurational whole in transcendence of elemental analysis.

By searching for truth in that synthesizing manner, Runge anticipated the *Gestalt* psychological approach to perception and cognition. Arising out of this synesthetic *Gestalt* theory and being a natural response to it, Runge's felt need for the *Gesamtkunstwerk* or total work of art as the only artistic vehicle serving all the requirements of that theory, appears to be the only possible quintessence of his artistic objectives. The resultant configurations being constellations of all the arts would, just as compound natural phenomena—and art to Runge was an intensified product of nature—exceed in significance the sum total of their parts. But despite the great efficacy with which Runge invested the synesthetic *Gestalt* aesthetics in fathoming the depth of subjective consciousness and the breadth of objective revelations, the answer to the ultimate secrets of both, according to him, had to remain forever locked in God's mysterious omniscience. And because also only God knew perfection, which was beyond man's capacity to reach, it appeared to Runge both fruitless and immoral to seek its attainment.

Out of these thoughts arises another original departure of Runge's theories, one which does not lack in fascination for the present-day student of art criticism. And that was, as we have seen, his suggestion of an art critique not based on standards of bravura, virtuosity, skill, accomplishment, and perfection relative to the finished product, but rather one founded on criteria predicated upon the right spirit, good will, and fine intentions of the artist and his capacity for expressing himself in sketchy, discursive, and fragmentary statements without detriment to their aesthetic validity.

Runge's work in color theory is of lasting practical value for the studio practitioner in its largely successful attempt at unification and sequential exposition of the many complex matters relating to color as artist's medium. More important in our context, Runge recognized the rich possibilities of color symbolism in its varied facets, including artistic expression through psychological color. In that respect we can see in Runge's work the anticipation of the theoretical bases of Symbolism and Expressionism, as in another, more technical aspect of his color theory, the germination of Impressionism.

Runge's pedagogical and art educational objectives are very startling in the modernity of their approach. He suggests an educational program which puts as much emphasis on the practice of art as it does on the training in perception and cognition. He counsels for the union of the various artistic disciplines; he calls for the cooperative workshop production and the incorporation of contemporary science and philosophy into the body of art theory. He urges putting an end to the stifling, unnatural, and unfunctional bifurcation of art into decorative and monumental branches, and he advocates a new role for that unified art as one not serving the jaded tastes of studio coterie and salon society, but rather the direct needs of the people at large and, above all, the private feelings and personal sense of civic responsibility of the individual artist. Thus Runge literally preempts the Bauhaus program.

By surprising us again and again with the beauty and logic of their inner consequence (despite their often naïve formulation and apparent disorder and informality in *Hinterlassene Schriften*), their timelessness for the contemporary reader, and their appropriateness for modern art, Runge's art theories dispel, in and by themselves, any notions that they may hold merely a historical or an antiquarian interest for us. Conversely, we must be all the more amazed about the virtual absence of any direct or even indirect influences they had upon the nineteenth century. Being free of pathos, arrogance, and exclusiveness, based on the highest ethical standards, dedicated to the service of humanity, and desirous of making art meaningful to all people after centuries of progressive estrangement from it, Runge's theories in their far-reaching and revolutionary consequences should, it seems, have appeared to his contemporaries and successors as an attractive alternative to the prevailing formal stalemate and spiritual ambivalence of German art during Runge's time, and as a very worthwhile and promising new course to pursue. However, Runge founded no school, despite the considerable, though temporary, excitement his ideas generated among his literary friends. He had no followers, and after his death his name fell into nearly total obscurity for the remainder of the nineteenth century; Runge died without heirs. I have enumerated several reasons for this astonishing fact. But after all is said, it seems to me that one simple phrase better describes Runge's posthumous fate than all the well-thought-out reasons and qualifications: "not all is possible at all times."

Conclusion

Had Runge lived in the late nineteenth century, his visions undoubtedly would have been much more compatible with the "climate of the times." Throughout the nineteenth century, but particularly in its closing phase, many artists worked, perhaps not knowing of Runge—except Friedrich (and presumably his friends Carus, Heinrich, Dahl and Kersting)—in partial, close, or nearly complete analogy to Runge's precepts. So, for example, in addition to the just-mentioned, such widely disparate artists as T. Rousseau, Millet, Van Gogh, Gauguin, Denis, Hodler, Munch, Bernard, Puvis de Chavannes, Moreau, and Redon, to name only a few very prominent names. Thus Runge may not have influenced nineteenth-century art, but it appears that his ideas were validated by consequent developments. The direct influence of Runge on Art Nouveau and Jugendstil and on such men as Morris, Horta, Van de Velde, and others, has been suggested but remains to be evaluated. The revolutionary formalistic-psychological aesthetics of Hildebrand, von Marées and, above all, Konrad Fiedler, at the turn of the century, reflect throughout Runge's penetrating insights. After his "discovery," Runge's influence on the twentieth century has been noted on Klee and Kandinsky. Marc worked in the closest correspondence to Runge's objectives. German Expressionism and mid-twentieth-century developments in the later and abstract phases of Expressionism corroborate the accuracy of many of his premises. But more than in any specific movements, currents, and schools, Runge's spirit is evident in the basic philosophical undercurrents of twentieth-century art. It seems that Runge's day, though late in coming, has arrived after all.

A SELECTED BIBLIOGRAPHY

I. WRITINGS BY RUNGE

Runge, Philipp Otto. *Farbenkugel,* oder Construction des Verhältnisses aller Mischungen der Farben zu einander und ihrer vollständigen Affinität; mit angehängtem Versuch einer Ableitung der Harmonie in den Zusammenstellungen der Farben. Hamburg: F. Perthes, 1810.

————. *Hinterlassene Schriften.* Vols. I, II. Hamburg: F. Perthes, 1840–1841; facsimile, Göttingen: Vandenhoeck & Ruprecht, 1965.

II. WRITINGS ABOUT RUNGE
(Chronological listing)

Note: The following chronologically ordered, selected listing contains the most important scholarly writings on the artist. The inordinately large number and variety of publications on Runge since his "discovery" by Alfred Lichtwark in 1893 have made qualitative bibliographical compilation a most difficult task. To this date we do not have a consummate bibliography on Runge. Works marked with an asterisk contain bibliographic attempts of varying excellence.

1821   Milarch, A. A. F. *Über Philipp Otto Runges "Vier Zeiten."* Berlin: Fr. Nicolaische Buchhandlung.

1844   Steffens, Heinrich. *Was Ich Erlebte, aus der Erinnerung niedergeschrieben.* 10 vols. Breslau: Max.

1857   Perthes, C. T. *Friedrich Perthes' Leben nach dessen schriftlichen und mündlichen Mitteilungen.* Vols. I, II. Gotha: F. A. Perthes.

1880   Rist, Johann Georg. *J. G. Rists' Lebenserinnerungen.* Vols. I, II. Gotha: G. Poel.

1884   Petrich, Herrmann. *Pommersche Lebens- und Landesbilder.* Part II. "Aus dem Zeitalter der Befreiung." Chap. V, Ph. O. Runge. Stettin: L. Sauniers' Buchhandlung.

1893   Lichtwark, Alfred. *Herrman Kauffmann und die Kunst in Hamburg von 1800–1850.* Munich: Verlagsanstalt für Kunst und Wissenschaft.

1895   ————. *Ph. O. Runge, Pflanzenstudien mit Schere und Papier.* Hamburg: Lutke & Wulff.

1907 Sulger-Gebing, E. *Philipp Otto Runge, Gedanken und Gedichte.* Munich: C. H. Beck.

1909 Aubert, *Runge und die Romantik.* Berlin.

1909 Krebs, Sigfried. *Philipp Otto Runge und Ludwig Tieck.* Inaugural dissertation, Freiburg im Breisgau.

1909 ————. *Ph. O. Runges Entwicklung unter dem Einflusse L. Tiecks. Studien zur Neueren Deutschen Literaturgeschichte*, I, 4, Heidelberg.

1909 Roch, Wolfgang. *Philipp Otto Runges Kunstanschauung nach seinen Hinterlassenen Schriften und ihr Verhältnis zur Frühromantik. Studien zur Deutschen Kunstgeschichte* III, Strassburg.

1910 Semrau, Max. "Zum Gedächtnis Ph. O. Runges." *Pommersche Jahrbücher* XI, pp. 224 ff.

1910 Dresdner, Albert. "Der Maler der Frühromantik (Philipp Otto Runge)." *Preussische Jahrbücher* (Berlin: Stilke) 139 (no. 1).

1911 Uhde-Bernays, H. "Ph. O. Runge und Klopstock." *Münchner Jahrbuch der bildenden Kunst*, Munich.

1913 Hancke, Erich. *Briefe von Ph. O. Runge.* Berlin: B. Cassirer.

1916* Pauli, Gustav. *Ph. O. Runges Zeichnungen und Scherenschnitte in der Kunsthalle zu Hamburg.* Berlin: B. Cassirer.

1916 Neumann, Carl. *Drei merkwürdige künstlerische Anregungen bei Runge, Manet, Goya.* Heidelberg: C. Winters Universitätsbuchhandlung.

1918 Pauli, Gustav. *Ph. O. Runge, Bilder und Bekenntnisse.* Berlin: Furche.

1923 Schmidt, Paul F. *Philipp Otto Runge, Sein Leben und sein Werk.* Leipzig: Insel.

1923 Benninghoff, Ludwig. *Philipp Otto Runge.* (3 folios with reproductions.) Hamburg: Hanseatischer Kunstverlag.

1923 Dirksen, Victor. *Ph. O. Runge, "Das Elternbild" und "Wir Drei."* Hamburg: Kunsthalle zu Hamburg Kleine Führer, no. 30.

1924 Mehnert, Arno. "Ph. O. Runge und der 'Morgen' aus seinem Zyklus 'Die Tageszeiten'." *Unser Pommerland, Monatsschrift für das Kulturleben der Heimat* (Stettin), Oct./Nov., pp. 333 ff.

1924 Scherping, Pauline. "Was Grossvater Runge seiner Enkelin erzählte, Erinnerungen von Ph. O. Runge." *Unser Pommerland, Monatsschrift für das Kulturleben der Heimat* (Stettin), Oct./Nov., pp. 346 ff.

1924 Schmidt, H. "Die Farbenlehre Ph. O. Runges und seine Bildgestalt." Inaugural dissertation, Kiel.

1925 Pauli, Gustav. *Die Kunst des Klassizismus und der Romantik.* Propyläen Kunstgeschichte XIV. Berlin: Propyläen.

1926 Schmidt, Paul F. "Ph. O. Runge der Maler der Romantik." *Velhagen und Klasings Monatshefte* (Leipzig) 40(1925/26), 2d vol., June.

1930 Grundy, J. B. C. "Tieck and Runge, A Study in the Relationship of Literature and Art in the Romantic Period with Special Reference to 'Franz Sternbald'." *Neue Heidelberger Jahrbücher* (Heidelberg: Koester).

1931 Schrade, Hubert. "Die romantische Idee von der Landschaft als höchstem Gegenstande Christlicher Kunst." *Neue Heidelberger Jahrbücher*, n.s., Jahrbuch 1931, Heidelberg.

1933 Börensen, Hans. "'Der Morgen' von Ph. O. Runge als eine Offenbarung vom Sinne der Kunst." *Niederdeutsche Welt* VIII, no. 12 (December): 335 ff.

1933 Eberlein, Kurt Karl. "Runges 'Tageszeiten', Das Gesamtkunstwerk der Romantik." *Der Wagen* (Lübeck: P. Brockhaus, F. Westphal).

1934 Böttcher, Otto. "Runge und die literarische Romantik." *Zeitschrift für Deutschkunde* (Leipzig-Berlin) 48, no. 8.

1935* Schmidt, Paul F. "Philipp Otto Runge, Maler." In Thieme-Becker *Künstlerlexikon*, vol 29. Leipzig: E. A. Seemann.

1937* Böttcher, Otto. *Philipp Otto Runge, Sein Leben, Wirken und Schaffen*. Hamburg: Friedrichsen, DeGruyter & Co.

1938 Gerlach, Hans Egon. *Philipp Otto Runge. Ein Versuch, zugleich Bekenntnis*. Berlin: Verlag Die Runde.

1940 Maltzahn, Hellmuth Freiherr von. *Philipp Otto Runges Briefwechsel mit Goethe*. Weimar: Verlag der Goethe Gesellschaft.

1940* Isermeyer, Ch. A. *Ph. O. Runge*. Berlin: Rembrandt.

1940* Degner, K. F. *Philipp Otto Runge, Briefe in der Urfassung*. Berlin: Nicolai.

1942 Simson, Otto Georg von. "Philipp Otto Runge and the Mythology of Landscape." *The Art Bulletin* 24:335–350.

1943 Dirksen, Victor. *Ph. O. Runge, Die Tageszeiten*. Der Kunstbrief, no. 14. Berlin: Gebrüder Mann.

1948 Einem, Herbert von. *Das Bildnis der Eltern von Philipp Otto Runge*. Der Kunstbrief, no. 45. Berlin: Gebrüder Mann.

1949* Ragué, Beatrix von. "Das Verhältnis von Kunst und Christentum bei Ph. O. Runge." Unpublished inaugural dissertation, Bonn.

1951* Waetzold, Stephan. "Ph. O. Runges 'Vier Zeiten'." Inaugural dissertation, Hamburg.

1959 Hebing, Julius. *Ph. O. Runge, Die Farbenkugel und andere Schriften zur Farbenlehre*. Stuttgart: Verlag Freies Geistesleben.

1959 Waetzold, Stephan. "Philipp Otto Runges 'Vier Zeiten' und ihre Konstruktionszeichnungen." Anzeiger des Germanischen Nationalmuseums, 1954–59, pp. 234–247.

1961 Berefelt, Gunnar. *Philipp Otto Runge zwischen Aufbruch und Opposition 1777–1802*. Stockholm: Almquist & Wiksell.

1962 ————. "Bemerkungen zu Ph. O. Runges Gestaltungstheorie." *Baltische Studien* (Hamburg: Chr. v.d. Rapp), n.s. 48 (1961): 51 ff.

1963* Langner, Johannes. *Philipp Otto Runge in der Hamburg Kunsthalle*. Bilderhefte der Hamburg Kunsthalle IV, Hamburg.

1964* Grützmacher, Curt. *Novalis und Philipp Otto Runge, Drei Zentralmotive und ihre Bedeutungssphäre: Die Blume—Das Kind—Das Licht*. Munich: Eidos.

III. ALPHABETICAL LISTING
(Including comparative literature)

Andrews, Keith. *The Nazarenes*. Oxford: Clarendon Press, 1964.

Antal, Friedrich. "Reflexions on Classicism and Romanticism." *Burlington Magazine* 66 (1935): 159–168: 67 (1936): 130–139; 77 (1940): 72–80; 78 (1941): 14–32.

Arnim, Achim von. *Achim von Arnims Werke*. Leipzig: Insel, 1911.

Aubert, *Runge und die Romantik*. Berlin, 1909.

Aurenhammer, Hans. *Lexikon der Christlichen Iconographie*. Vienna: Hollinek, 1962.

Babbitt, Irving. *Rousseau and Romanticism*. Boston: Houghton Mifflin Co., 1919.

Barker, C. J. *Pre-Requisites for the Study of Jacob Böhme*. London: J. M. Wathins, 1920.

Barzun, Jacques. *Classic, Romantic, Modern*. New York: Doubleday & Co., 1961.

Beenken, Herman. *Das Neunzehnte Jahrhundert in der Deutschen Kunst, Aufgaben und Gehalte, Versuch einer Rechenschaft*. Munich: Bruckmann, 1944.

Bell, Clive. *Landmarks in Nineteenth Century Painting*. New York: Harcourt, Brace & Co., 1927.

Benninghoff, Ludwig. *Philipp Otto Runge*. (3 folios with reproductions.) Hamburg: Hanseatischer Kunstverlag, 1923.

Benz, Richard. *Die Deutsche Romantik*. Leipzig: Reclam, 1937.

Berefelt, Gunnar. *Philipp Otto Runge zwischen Aufbruch und Opposition 1777–1802*. Stockholm: Almquist & Wiksell, 1961.

————. "Bemerkungen zu Ph. O. Runges Gestaltungstheorie." *Baltische Studien* (Hamburg: Chr. v.d. Rapp, 1962), n.s. 48 (1961): 51 ff.

Bietack, Wilhelm. *Lebenslehre und Weltanschauung der Jüngeren Romantik*. Leipzig: Reclam, 1936.

Böhme, Jacob. *Theosophia Revelata, oder Alle Göttlichen Schriften Jacob Böhmes von Alt-seidenberg*. Stuttgart: Frommann, 1955.

Börensen, Hans. "'Der Morgen' von Ph. O. Runge als eine Offenbarung vom Sinne der Kunst." *Niederdeutsche Welt* (Lübeck-Hamburg-Bremen) VIII, no. 12 (Dec. 1933): 335 ff.

Böttcher, Otto. "Runge und die literarische Romantik." *Zeitschrift für Deutschkunde* (Leipzig-Berlin) 48, no. 8 (1934).

————. *Philipp Otto Runge, Sein Leben, Wirken und Schaffen*. Hamburg: Friedrichsen, DeGruyter & Co., 1937.

Brentano, Clemens. *Werke*. Munich: Hanser, 1963.

Brieger, L. *Die Romantische Malerei*. Berlin: Deutsche Buchgemeinschaft, 1926.

Brion, Marcel. *Romantic Art*. New York: McGraw-Hill, 1960.

————. *Art of the Romantic Era*. New York: F. A. Praeger, 1966.

Canaday, John. *Mainstreams of Modern Art*. New York: Holt, Rinehart & Winston, 1959.

Carus, Gustav. *Gesammelte Schriften*. Berlin: Keiper, 1938.

Clark, Kenneth. *The Gothic Revival*. New York: Scribners, 1950.

————. "The Romantic Movement." Introduction to Catalogue, The Tate Gallery, London, 1959.

————. *Landscape into Art*. Boston: The Beacon Press, 1961.

Claudius, Mathias. *Sämtliche Werke des Wandsbecker Bothen*. Hamburg: Bode, 1871.

Coplestone, Frederick. *A History of Philosophy*. London: Burnes, Oates & Washbourne, 1963.

Courthion, Pierre. *Romanticism in Art*. Cleveland: The World Publishing Co., 1961.

Degner, K. F. *Philipp Otto Runge, Briefe in der Urfassung*. Berlin: Nicolai, 1940.

Deusch, W. R. *Malerei der Deutschen Romantiker und ihrer Zeitgenossen*. Berlin: Genius, 1937.

Dirksen, Victor. *Ph. O. Runge, "Das Elternbild" und "Wir Drei."* Hamburg: Kunsthalle zu Hamburg Kleine Führer, no. 30, 1923.

————. *Ph. O. Runge, Die Tageszeiten*. Der Kunstbrief, no. 14. Berlin: Gebrüder Mann, 1943.

Dresdner, Albert. "Der Maler der Frühromantik (Philipp Otto Runge)." *Preussische Jahrbücher* (Berlin: Stilke) 139, no. 1 (1910).

Eberlein, K. K. *Goethe und die bildende Kunst der Romantik*. Jahrbuch der Goethegesellschaft. Weimar, 1928.

————. "Runges 'Tageszeiten,' Das Gesamtkunstwerk der Romantik." *Der Wagen* (Lübeck: P. Brockhaus, F. Westphal), 1933.

Ebstein, Erich. *Tuberkulose als Schicksal, Eine Sammlung pathographischer Skizzen von Calvin bis Klabund, 1502–1928*. Stuttgart: Ecke, 1932.

BIBLIOGRAPHY

Einem, Herbert von. *Caspar David Friedrich*. Berlin: K. Lemmer, 1938.

―――. *Das Bildnis der Eltern von Philipp Otto Runge*. Der Kunstbrief, no. 45. Berlin: Gebrüder Mann, 1948.

Eitner, Lorenz. "The Open Window and the Storm-Tossed Boat." *The Art Bulletin 37* (1955): 281–290.

Ermatinger, Emil. *Das Erbe der Alten*. Leipzig: Reclam, 1935.

Ferguson, George. *Signs and Symbols in Christian Art*. New York: Oxford University Press, 1961.

Fichte, J. G. *Sämtliche Werke*. Berlin: Veit, 1846.

Fischer, Otto. *Caspar David Friedrich. Die Romantische Landschaft; Dokumente und Bilder*. Stuttgart: Strecker & Schröder, 1922.

―――. *Geschichte der Deutschen Malerei*. Munich: Bruckmann, 1956.

Friedländer, M. J. *Landscape, Portrait, Still-Life*. New York: Schocken Books, 1963.

Geese, Walter. "Die Heroische Landschaft nach 1800." *Studien zur Deutschen Kunstgeschichte* (Strassburg), no. 201 (1917).

Gerlach, Hans Egon. *Phillip Otto Runge. Ein Versuch, zugleich Bekenntnis*. Berlin: Verlag Die Runde, 1938.

Gleckner, R. F., and Enscoe, G. E. *Romanticism, Points of View*. Englewood Cliffs, N.J.: Prentice-Hall, 1966.

Goethe, J. W. *Sämtliche Werke*. Stuttgart: Cotta, 1840.

―――. *Schriften zur Kunst*. Zurich: Artemis, 1954.

Grundy, J. B. C. "Tieck and Runge, A Study in the Relationship of Literature and Art in the Romantic Period with Special Reference to 'Franz Sternbald'." *Neue Heidelberger Jahrbücher* (Heidelberg: Koester), 1930.

Grützmacher, Curt. *Novalis und Philipp Otto Runge, Drei Zentralmotive und ihre Bedeutungssphäre: Die Blume—Das Kind—Das Licht*. Munich: Eidos, 1964.

Gurlitt, V. *Die Deutsche Kunst seit 1800*. Berlin: Bondi, 1924.

Hamann, Richard. *Die Deutsche Malerei im 19. Jahrhundert*. Leipzig, 1914.

Hancke, Erich. *Briefe von Ph. O. Runge*. Berlin: B. Cassirer, 1913.

Hauser, Arnold. *A Social History of Art*, vols. 3, 4. New York: Random House, 1962.

Haym, Rudolf. *Die Romantische Schule*. Berlin: Weidmannsche Buchhandlung, 1906.

Hebing, Julius. *Ph. O. Runge, Die Farbenkugel und andere Schriften zur Farbenlehre*. Stuttgart: Verlag Freies Geistesleben, 1959.

Hegel, G. W. F. *Werke*. Berlin: Duncker, 1840.

Heise, C. G. *Deutsche Zeichner des XIX und XX Jahrhunderts*. Berlin: Gebrüder Mann, 1946.

Hildebrandt, Hans. *Die Kunst des 19. und 20. Jahrhunderts. Handbuch der Kunstwissenschaft*, vol. 30. Potsdam: Verlagsgesellschaft Athenaion, 1924.

Hintze, Charlotte. "Kopenhagen und die Deutsche Malerei um 1800." Inaugural dissertation, Würzburg, 1937.

Hofman, Werner. *The Earthly Paradise, Art in the 19th Century*. New York: G. Braziller, 1961.

Höhn, Heinrich, "Studien zur Entwicklung der Münchner Landschaftsmalerei vom Ende des 18. und Anfang des 19. Jahrhunderts." *Studien zur Deutschen Kunstgeschichte* (Strassburg), no. 108 (1909).

Holt, Elizabeth G. *From the Classicists to the Impressionists, Art and Architecture in the Nineteenth Century*. New York: Doubleday & Co., 1966.

Huch, Ricarda. *Blütezeit der Romantik*. Leipzig: Haessel, 1905.

―――. *Ausbreitung und Verfall der Romantik*. Leipzig: Haessel, 1905.

Isermeyer, Ch. A. *Ph. O. Runge*. Berlin: Rembrandt, 1940.

Kandinsky, Wassili. *Über das Geistige in der Kunst.* Munich: Piper & Co., 1912.

———. *Punkt und Linie zu Fläche.* 3d ed. Bern-Bumplitz, 1955.

———. *Essays über Kunst und Künstler.* Teufen: Niggli & Verkauf, 1955.

Klee, Paul. *Pedagogisches Skizzenbuch.* Munich: Langer, 1925.

Kleinmayr, Hugo. *Die Deutsche Romantik und die Landschaftsmalerei.* Strassburg: Heitz, 1912.

Kluckhohn, Paul. *Das Ideengut der Deutschen Romantik.* Tübingen: Niemeyer, 1953.

Krebs, Sigfried. "Philipp Otto Runge und Ludwig Tieck." Inaugural dissertation, Freiburg im Breisgau, 1909.

———. *P. O. Runges Entwicklung unter dem Einflusse L. Tiecks. Studien zur Neueren Deutschen Literaturgeschichte* (Heidelberg), 1, 4 (1909).

Künstle, Karl. *Ikonographie der Christlichen Kunst.* Freiburg: Herder & Co., 1926.

Langner, Johannes. *Philipp Otto Runge in der Hamburg Kunsthalle.* Bilderhefte der Hamburg Kunsthalle IV, Hamburg, 1963.

Lankheit, Klaus. "Die Frühromantik und die Grundlagen der Gegenstandslosen Malerei." *Neue Heidelberger Jahrbücher,* 1951.

Lavater, J. C. *J. C. Lavaters Physiognomische Fragmente zur Beförderung der Menschenkenntnis und der Menschenliebe.* Vienna: Solinger, 1829.

Lessing, G. E. *Lessings Werke.* Stuttgart: Göschen, 1874.

Lichtwark, Alfred. *Herrman Kauffmann und die Kunst in Hamburg von 1800–1850.* Munich: Verlagsanstalt für Kunst und Wissenschaft, 1893.

———. *Ph. O. Runge, Pflanzenstudien mit Schere und Papier.* Hamburg: Lutke & Wulff, 1895.

Lotze, Hermann. *Geschichte der Aesthetik in Deutschland.* Munich: Cotta, 1868.

Lovejoy, Arthur. *Essays in the History of Ideas.* New York: Putnam & Sons, 1960.

Lurker, Manfred. *Symbol, Mythos und Legende in der Kunst (Die Symbolische Aussage in Malerei, Plastik und Architektur). Studien zur Deutschen Kunstgeschichte* (Strassburg) 314 (1958).

Maltzahn, Hellmuth Freiherr von. *Philipp Otto Runges Briefwechsel mit Goethe.* Weimar: Verlag der Goethe Gesellschaft, 1940.

Martini, Fritz. *Deutsche Literaturgeschichte.* Stuttgart: Kröner, 1960.

Mehnert, Arno. "Ph. O. Runge und der 'Morgen' aus seinem Zyklus 'die Tageszeiten'." *Unser Pommerland, Monatschrift für das Kulturleben der Heimat* (Stettin), Oct./Nov., 1924, pp. 333 ff.

Meyer, F. J. L. *Skizzen zu einem Gemälde von Hamburg,* vols. I, II. Hamburg: Nestler, 1800–1802.

Milarch, A. A. F. *Über Philipp Otto Runges "Vier Zeiten."* Berlin: F. Nicolaische Buchhandlung, 1821.

Morris, William. *The Decorative Arts, their Relation to Modern Life and Progress.* Boston: Roberts Brothers, 1878.

———. *On Art and Socialism.* London: Lehmann, 1947.

Munsell, A. H. *A Color Notation.* An Illustrated System Defining all Colors and their Relations by measured Scales of Hue, Value and Chroma. 11th ed. Baltimore: Munsell Color Company, 1961.

Müller, Andreas. *Kunstanschauung der Frühromantik.* Leipzig: Reclam, 1931.

Negus, Kenneth. "Novalis und Philipp Otto Runge." Book Reviews. *German Quarterly,* Spring 1966.

Neumann, Carl. *Drei merkwürdige künstlerische Anregungen bei Runge, Manet, Goya.* Heidelberg: Winter, 1916.

Newton, Eric. *The Romantic Rebellion.* New York: St. Martin's Press, 1962.

Nochlin, Linda, *Realism and Tradition in Art 1848–1900.* Englewood Cliffs, N. J.: Prentice-Hall, 1966.

———. *Impressionism and Post-Impressionism 1874–1904.* Englewood Cliffs, N. J.: Prentice-Hall, 1966.

Novalis (Friedrich von Hardenberg). *Novalis Werke.* Stuttgart: Hädecke, 1960.

Novotny, Fritz. *Painting and Sculpture in Europe, 1780–1880.* Baltimore: Penguin Books, 1960.

Pauli, Gustav. *Ph. Otto Runges Zeichnungen und Scherenschnitte in der Kunsthalle zu Hamburg.* Berlin: B. Cassirer, 1916.

———. *Ph. O. Runge, Bilder und Bekenntnisse.* Berlin: Furche, 1918.

———. *Die Kunst des Klassizismus und der Romantik.* Propyläen Kunstgeschichte, XIV. Berlin: Propyläen, 1925.

Pauli, Gustav, and Dehio, Georg. *Das Neunzehnte Jahrhundert.* Geschichte der Deutschen Kunst, vol. 4. Berlin: DeGruyter, 1934.

Pelles, Geraldine. *Art, Artists and Society, Origins of a Modern Dilemma, Painting in England and France 1750–1850.* Englewood Cliffs, N. J.: Prentice-Hall, 1963.

Perthes, C. T. *Friedrich Perthes' Leben nach dessen schriftlichen und mündlichen Mitteilungen.* Vols. I, II. Gotha: F. A. Perthes, 1857.

Petrich, Herrmann. *Pommerische Lebens- und Landesbilder.* Part II. "Aus dem Zeitalter der Befreiung," Chap. V, Ph. O. Runge. Stettin: L. Sauniers' Buchhandlung, 1884–1887.

Pevsner, N.; Evers, H. G.; Besset, M.; Grote, L. *et al. Historismus und bildende Kunst.* Studien zur Kunst des neunzehnten Jahrhunderts, Vol. I. Munich: Forschungsunternehmen der Fritz Thyssen Stiftung, Arbeitskreis Kunstgeschichte, Prestel Verlag, 1965.

Ragué, Beatrix von. "Das Verhältnis von Kunst und Christentum bei Ph. O. Runge." Unpublished inaugural dissertation, Bonn, 1949.

Reinhardt, Kurt. *The Existentialist Revolt.* New York: Ungar, 1960.

Riegl, Alois. *Stilfragen, Grundlegungen zu einer Geschichte der Ornamentik.* Berlin: Schmidt & Co., 1893.

Rist, Johann. *J. G. Rists' Lebenserinnerungen.* Vols. I, II. Gotha: Poel, 1880.

Roch, Wolfgang. *Philipp Otto Runges Kunstanschauung nach seinen Hinterlassenen Schriften und ihr Verhältnis zur Frühromantik. Studien zur Deutschen Kunstgeschichte* (Strassburg) III (1909).

Russell, Bertrand. *A History of Western Philosophy.* New York: Simon & Schuster, 1946.

Scheffler, Karl. *Verwandlungen des Barocks in der Kunst des Neunzehnten Jahrhunderts.* Vienna: Gallus, 1947.

Schelling, F. W. J. *Schellings Werke.* Leipzig-Vienna: Bibliographisches Institut, 1907.

Scherping, Pauline. "Was Grossvater Runge seiner Enkelin erzählte, Erinnerungen von Ph. O. Runge." *Unser Pommerland, Monatsschrift für das Kulturleben der Heimat* (Stettin), Oct./Nov., (1924), 346 ff.

Schiller, Friedrich. *Werke.* Weimar: Böhlaus, Nachfolger, 1964.

Schlegel, Friedrich. *Sämtliche Werke.* Leipzig: Reclam, Jr., 1910.

Schlegel, Friedrich and A. W. *Athenäum.* Stuttgart: Cotta, 1960.

Schleiermacher, Friedrich. *Über die Religion, Reden an die Gebildeten unter ihren Verächtern.* Leipzig: Kröner, 1907.

Schmidt, H. "Die Farbenlehre Ph. O. Runges und seine Bildgestalt." Inaugural disertation, Kiel, 1924.

Schmidt, Paul F. *Philipp Otto Runge, Sein Leben und sein Werk.* Leipzig: Insel, 1923.

———. "Ph. O. Runge der Maler der Romantik." *Velhagen und Klasings Monatshefte* (Leipzig) 40 (1925/26), 2d vol., June 1926.

———. *Deutsche Malerei um 1800*. Munich: Piper & Co., 1928.

———. "Philipp Otto Runge, Maler." In Thieme-Becker *Künstlerlexikon*, vol. 29. Leipzig: E. A. Seemann, 1935.

Schöne, Wolfgang. *Über das Licht in der Malerei*. Berlin: Gebrüder Mann, 1954.

Schopenhauer, Arthur. *Sämtliche Werke*. Leipzig: Reclam, Jr., 1910.

Schrade, Hubert. "Die Romantische Idee von der Landschaft." *Neue Heidelberger Jahrbücher*, 1931.

Seiffert-Wattenberg. *Deutsche Maler von Runge bis Menzel, 1800–1850*. Munich: Bruckmann, 1934.

Semrau, Max. "Zum Gedächtnis Ph. O. Runges." *Pommersche Jahrbücher* XI (1910): 224 ff.

Sherrington, Charles. *Goethe on Nature and on Science*. Cambridge: The University Press, 1949.

Simson, Otto Georg von. "Philipp Otto Runge and the Mythology of Landscape." *The Art Bulletin* 24 (1942): 335–350.

Steffens, Heinrich. *Was Ich Erlebte, aus der Erinnerung niedergeschrieben*. 10 vols. Breslau: Max, 1844.

———. *Was Ich Erlebte*. Munich: Winkler, 1956.

Stein, Wilhelm. *Die Erneuerung der Heroischen Landschaft nach 1800. Studien zur Deutschen Kunstgeschichte* (Strassburg), no. 201, 1917.

Stelzer, Otto. *Die Vorgeschichte der Abstrakten Kunst. Denkmodelle und Vor-Bilder*. Munich: Piper & Co., 1964.

Stöcker, Helene. *Zur Kunstanschauung des XVII Jahrhunderts*. Berlin: Meyer & Müller, 1904.

Strich, Fritz. *Deutsche Klassik und Romantik*. Munich: Meyer & Issen, 1922.

Sulger-Gebing, E. *Philipp Otto Runge, Gedanken und Gedichte*. Munich: C. H. Beck, 1907.

———. *Die Brüder Wilhelm und Friedrich Schlegel in ihrem Verhältnis zur bildenden Kunst*. Forschung zur Neueren Literaturgeschichte, vol. III. Munich, 1957.

Thieme, U., and Becker, F. (later by H. Vollmer), eds. *Allgemeines Lexikon der bildenden Künstler von der Antike bis zur Gegenwart*. 37 vols. Leipzig: E. A. Seemann, 1907–1950.

Tieck, Ludwig. *Tiecks Werke*. Leipzig-Vienna: Bibliographisches Institut, n.d.

Tschudi, H. von. *Die Deutsche Jahrhundertausstellung zu Berlin, 1906*. Munich: Bruckmann, 1906.

Uhde-Bernays, H. "Ph. O. Runge und Klopstock." *Münchner Jahrbuch der bildenden Kunst*, Munich, 1911.

Ullmann, R., and Gotthard, H. *Geschichte des Begriffes "Romantisch" in Deutschland, vom ersten Aufkommen des Wortes bis ins dritte Jahrzehnt des neunzehnten Jahrhunderts*. Berlin: Ebering, 1927.

Venturi, Lionel. *History of Art Criticism*. New York: E. P. Dutton & Co., 1936.

Volbehr, T. *Verlangen nach einer neuen deutschen Kunst: ein Verzeichnis des 18. Jahrhunderts*. Leipzig: Dietrichs, 1901.

Wackenroder, W. H. *Werke und Briefe*. Jena: Diederichs, 1910.

Waetzold, Stephan. "Ph. O. Runges 'Vier Zeiten'." Inaugural dissertation, Hamburg, 1951.

———. *Philipp Otto Runges "Vier Zeiten" und ihre Konstruktionszeichnungen*. Anzeiger des Germanischen Nationalmuseums, 1954–59, pp. 234–247.

Winckelmann, Johann J. *Gedanken über die Nachahmung der griechischen Werke in der Malerei und Bildhauerkunst. Deutsche Literaturdenkmale des 18. und 19. Jahrhunderts*, vol. 20. Stuttgart: Seuffert, 1885.

Windelband, Wilhelm. *A History of Philosophy*. London: Macmillan & Co., 1898.

Wingler, H. M. *Das Bauhaus, 1919–1933, Weimar, Dessau, Berlin*. Wiesbaden: Gebrüder Rasch & Co. & M. DuMont Schauberg, 1962.

Zeitler, Rudolf. "Klassizismus und Utopia." Inaugural dissertation, Stockholm, 1954.

———. *Die Kunst des 19. Jahrhunderts*. Propyläen Kunstgeschichte, Vol. 11. Berlin: Propyläen Verlag, 1966.

IV. FICTION ABOUT RUNGE

Meichner, Fritz. *Wir Drei, eine Runge Novelle*. Berlin: Union, 1962.

INDEX OF NAMES

INDEX

INDEX OF SUBJECTS